Trails of Blood
Legends of the Vampire

BR Williams

Roswell Publishing

Text © 2023 BR Williams and Roswell Publishing.

The rights of BR Williams identified as the originator of this work has been asserted by them in accordance with the Copyright, Designs and Patents Act 1988.

All rights reserved. No part of this publication may be reproduced, stored in a retrieval system, or transmitted in any form or by any means electronic, mechanical, photocopying, recording or otherwise, without prior permission.

ISBN: 9798864369838

Cover image: akadarcee @ Pixabay

For rights and other permissions, please contact Rachael at: rae@raegee.co.uk

Chapter 1......Vampires ... 2
Chapter 2.....Vampires of the Ancient World ... 11
Chapter 3.....Vampires of the Middle Ages ... 22
Chapter 4.....The Victorian Vampire ... 32
Chapter 5.....Slavic Vampires ... 42
Chapter 6.....Asian Vampires ... 51
Chapter 7.....Vampires of Africa and the Middle East ... 65
Chapter 8.....Vampires of North America ... 73
Chapter 9.....Vampires of South America ... 88
Chapter 10.....Vampires in Pop Cultures ... 98
Chapter 11.....The Modern Vampire ... 110
Chapter 12.....Medical Explanations ... 119
Chapter 13.....The Hunters ... 127

Introduction

Vampires have long been a source of fascination and dread. From the earliest recorded accounts to our modern-day stories, vampires have been a part of human culture in one form or another. Throughout history, vampires have been portrayed in literature, film, television, and more recently, video games and comic books.

This book will explore the history of vampires and their manifestations in different cultures and periods. We will look at how vampires have been depicted in different media, their influence on popular culture, and the evolution of vampire mythology over time. We will also examine how vampires have been used as a metaphor for our fears and anxieties and how they have been used to address issues of gender, sexuality, and race.

In this book, you will find a comprehensive overview of vampires throughout history and a deeper exploration of how they have been depicted in culture. Whether you are a fan of vampire fiction or simply curious about the history of these creatures, this book will offer an intriguing look at one of the most enduring cultural icons of all time.

Chapter 1: Vampires

Vampires are mysterious creatures that have played a role in world folklore since ancient times. They are both frightening and alluring simultaneously. In the past, the vampire was not glamorized as it is today and served as a warning to early people. Today, the vampire is still an essential archetype within modern society.

Energetically, there are those who may absorb or steal energy from others. They are called energy vampires. For example, when you are tired, and someone continues to talk and hold your attention they are actively draining your energy. But this is only part of the archetype. Vampires represent both shadow and light.

Blood is the preferred source of nourishment for vampires. Blood represents the life force or energy. Blood played an essential role in many early cultures. Consider the blood sacrifices of the Meso-American cultures. For the ancient Greeks blood represented one's temperament and was equated with warmth and cordiality.[1] With this in mind further, consider the practice of bloodletting as a means of healing.

Blood may also symbolize love and rage. Consider the phrase "*My blood was boiling*." Blood is pumped by the heart, the center of strong emotions. In this, the vampire is viewed as pale and emotionless when seen in the light yet, in the darkness warm and emotional.

The Beginning
The history of vampires is a centuries-old phenomenon that has been present in various cultures around the world. The earliest recorded vampire-like creatures can be found in ancient Mesopotamian, Greco-Roman, and Indian folklore. They were often described as creatures of the night that fed on human blood. In the Middle Ages, vampires began to appear in

---

[1] Book of Symbols by the Archive for research in Archetypal Symbolism

literature, in works such as "The Vampire of Padova" and "The Vampire of Nuremberg". These stories often featured a nobleman who was cursed with an immortal life of bloodsucking.

In the 19th century, author Bram Stoker introduced Count Dracula in his novel Dracula. This character is one of the most iconic vampires in literature and has been adapted into countless films and other media. In the 20th century, vampires began to appear in popular culture, often portrayed as attractive, romantic figures with superhuman powers. Today, vampires continue to be popular in literature and film, as well as in television series, comic books, and video games.

Today the standard view of the vampire is akin to a soap opera. Modern vampires are sexy, typically very wealthy, and have serious drama. I mean honestly, if I lived for centuries, I'd be putting back a few dollars myself. I'd also have all the time in the world to perfect my smokey-eye look. It is reasonable that someone would be pretty mad at me for centuries to hold a grudge. But historically, society has not always been in love with vampires. Actually, they were quite frightened.

Identification

Through the centuries many methods have evolved to identify a vampire formally. Most legends relate that a vampire is a human, and without immediate identifying attributes, it was necessary to invent ways to identify them. Numerous cultures invented rituals to identify a vampire. One such method involved leading a virgin boy through a graveyard or church grounds on a virgin stallion to find a vampire's grave. The premise was that the horse would shy away from a vampire's grave. Normally, a black horse was required, however, in Albania, it needed to be white. According to folklore, holes that had appeared in the ground over a grave were a sign of a vampire grave.

Contrary to previously held beliefs, corpses thought to be vampires were commonly described as having a healthier appearance than expected. They were plump and showed little or no signs of decomposition. In some cases, when suspected graves were opened, villagers even described the corpse as having fresh blood from a victim all over its face. Today, even lay people are aware of the decomposition process of the recently deceased. In the absence of embalming, these are all normal attributes and should be expected.

In the days before embalming, bodies were buried in permeable wooden boxes. Under such conditions, the natural decaying process would cause a gradual bloating of the body. This was due to the release of gases. Further, it could even cause blood to appear from the corpse's mouth as the lungs are squeezed during the natural process. Adding to the hysteria, driving a stake through the chest of a body in this state can cause it to release an unnerving cry. This is not because the person is still alive, but because gases are being forced outwards due to the force of the stake.

The evidence that a vampire was active in a location included the death of cattle, sheep, relatives, or neighbors. This could include rampant diseases such as tuberculosis or even the black plague. According to folklore, vampires also made their presence felt through minor poltergeist-styled activity. For example, flinging stones on roofs, moving everyday objects around the house, or applying physical pressure on people in their sleep.[2]

Appearances are Everything

In stark contrast to the modern gorgeous creature of the night, vampires in early European folklore were gruesome. As vampires were undead creatures, it is unsurprising that early descriptions report them bloated, ruddy, or purplish in color, and blood spilled from their mouths and noses. In many areas of Eastern Europe, so-called "vampire graves" are still unearthed, containing the dead spiked to the ground and with a brick lodged in their mouth. In some instances, the body is

---

2   Bunson, Matthew (1993). The Vampire Encyclopedia. London: Thames & Hudson.

decapitated to prevent it from rising from the grave.

The look of vampires has altered throughout history. and also varies depending on the area of the world from which the legends originate. Some vampires are depicted as having a long tongue to suck human blood while others can rip their own body in half to take flight and kill. The sexy gothic vampires that are quite popular in literature and movies appear a certain way as well yet has very little to do with historical accounts.

In more modern folklore, vampires are often depicted as pale, undead (yet gorgeous) creatures with sharp, pointed teeth and long, dark hair. They are typically portrayed as having a "gothic" look, wearing dark cloaks, and sometimes having a dark, shadowy complexion. Their nails and eyes may be red or black, depending on the story, and they often possess the ability to transform into a bat or wolf. Vampires may also be described as having a supernatural aura, with their presence being described as bringing a chill to the air. In some stories, they have the ability to hypnotize people or cast spells. Modern folkloric vampires are also thought to have an aversion to garlic, crosses, and holy water.

Making of Modern Vampires

Thank you, Mr. Stoker. In the nineteenth century, many people became enthralled by horror stories. Despite all the scientific advances happening, society was fascinated with the supernatural. During the 1800s, vampires were generally viewed with fear and superstition. Folkloric tales of blood-drinking creatures of the night had been circulating in Europe for centuries. Stories of vampires became even more popular in the 19th century thanks to the publication of Bram Stoker's novel *Dracula* in 1897.[3]

Dracula significantly impacted how the vampire is viewed,

---

[3] *Dracula* tells the story of a vampire named Count Dracula and his attempt to move from Transylvania to England in order to find new blood and spread the undead curse. The novel follows a group of characters as they attempt to stop Dracula and save the world from his evil. See Chapter 5 Victorian Vampire.

both in literature and popular culture. The novel popularized the vampire as a powerful and sinister figure who drinks blood and is capable of immense strength and seduction. Stoker's vampire has come to be seen as the archetypal vampire of literature, with many of his characteristics and traits being replicated in subsequent works based around vampires. Further, Stoker's novel was also influential in the development of vampire films. Many took inspiration from his novel's themes and characters. For example, the iconic figures of Count Dracula, Van Helsing, and Mina Harker have become staples of vampire films, with each character often being adapted to fit the particular needs of the plotline. Additionally, the narrative's setting of Transylvania has become an iconic location for vampire movies, with many taking place in the region.

Dracula helped to create many familiar vampire tropes in popular culture today. Stoker's novel features vampires that can change shape, have supernatural strength, and be killed with a wooden stake. These images are still seen in vampire films and literature today and can be traced back to his work. Bram Stoker's *Dracula* significantly influenced how a vampire is viewed today. His novel popularized the vampire as a powerful and dangerous creature and created many of the familiar vampire tropes that are still seen in literature and film today.

Creating a Vampire

Now that we know how vampires looked, the question remains of how they were created. Modern vampire lore suggests that a lonely vampire seeks out a companion and after drinking their blood, sometimes feeding the victim their own blood, a new vampire is created. Oh, how sweet. But no, not in traditional folklore. Vampires were considered the remnants of some evil being, a witch, or even a poor soul who committed suicide. Sometimes a wicked entity would jump into a dead body to drive it around for a while and suck blood. If a wretched vampire did bite someone, think of it more along the lines of a zombie, you were merely food but now you will be the predator as you morph into a vampire.

Conversely, some folklore puts forth that Vampires are not created, they are born. It is believed that vampires were born through a blood curse passed down through generations. The blood curse is often associated with a person or family cursed by a powerful witch or sorcerer. This curse is believed to be a way to transform a regular human into a vampire. Vampires have a variety of supernatural powers, such as the ability to shape-shift, control the weather, and hypnotize humans. Even more frightening than encountering a vampire was being accused of vampirism. It carried a penalty of death!

Do Vampires *Need* a Coffin?

One of the most well-known possessions of the vampire is his coffin. As sunlight can allegedly destroy a vampire, many are reported to sleep inside a coffin. As such, the coffin has become an iconic part of vampire folklore and is still used in modern vampire fiction. It is a powerful symbol of death, protection, and mystery. Additionally, it helps create the atmosphere of terror and suspense integral to the vampire genre.

Coffins have been a part of vampire folklore for centuries. The first mention of a vampire using a coffin appears in the 18th-century novel The *Vampyre* by John William Polidori. In this story, the vampire uses a coffin to travel from place to place and to hide during the day.[4] The popularity of coffins in vampire folklore began to surge in the 19th century. This is due in large part to the emergence of the vampire in popular culture during this time. Gothic literature and horror films featured vampires sleeping in coffins, and this imagery helped cement the idea of vampires and coffins in the public consciousness.

Before coffins, vampires may have slept in crypts, crypt-like spaces, or other hidden places such as underground caverns. They also may have slept in their graves as many believed that vampires were undead and rose from the grave during the night.

---

[4] John William Polidori, "The Vampyre," in Lord Byron's Novel: The Evening Land, ed. Malcolm Kelsall (Oxford: Oxford University Press, 1976), pp. 1-11.

The coffin, crypt, and grave are all seen as symbols of death, and this symbolism has been used in vampire fiction to represent the death-like state of vampires when they are dormant during the day. They serve as places of refuge and protection for the vampire. Such places are used to hide from the sunlight and avoid human detection.

Do Not Cross the Stream!

Water is at the center of many legends regarding evil. Porches in the American South are typically painted blue, representing water, as it is believed that evil cannot cross water. It is little wonder that vampire folklore also has similar legends regarding water. The myth that vampires cannot cross running water is ancient and is found in many cultures and religions around the world. It is rooted in ancient beliefs. According to the legend, vampires are unable to cross over any body of water that is running, such as a river, stream, or even a waterfall. This is said to be because water is a symbol of purity and divinity, and vampires are considered to be creatures of the night and impure. In some versions, the vampire is unable to cross due to the power of the water, while in other tales, the vampire is too afraid to attempt it. In some legends, the vampire is even believed to be incapable of flying over running water, as the power of the water prevents them from doing so.

This idea of the vampire's inability to cross running water is still in popular culture today. Just as elements from *Dracula*, the legend of running water is often used in films, television shows, and books, in some cases, it is an obstacle for the vampire, preventing them from reaching their destination or victim. In other scenarios, it is used as an explanation as to how the vampire is able to be killed, as they are unable to escape across the running water. Whether it is used as an obstacle for the vampire or as an explanation for their death, it remains a curious part of vampire lore and is a concept with which many people are familiar.

Vampire Prevention

While folklore points to running water as an obstacle for the vampire, there are other methods of prevention. While one can prevent a vampire attack, it is best to avert a loved one from becoming a vampire in the first place. Cultural rituals that were intended to prevent a newly departed loved one from transforming into an undead revenant arose in the past. For example, burying a corpse upside-down was common. Additionally, the practice of placing earthly objects, such as scythes or sickles, near the grave in order to satisfy all possible demons so they would not enter the body. Furthermore, such goods would appease the dead so they would not wish to rise from its coffin.[5]

Another method commonly practiced in early Europe included severing the tendons at the knees. Some placed poppy seeds, millet, or sand on the grave site of a presumed vampire. This practice was intended to keep the vampire entertained all night counting the fallen grains. This act suggested an association of vampires with OCD (Obsessive Compulsive Disorder).[6] Such safeguards were not always adequate, and some corpses became blood-sucking monsters. Or so the townsfolk believed.

The prevailing belief is that the best way to prevent a vampire from attacking is to take precautionary measures and be aware of your surroundings. Make sure to keep all windows and doors locked at night and avoid going out alone after dark. If a person must be out after dark, bringing a friend and staying in well-lit, populated areas are thought wise. This is honestly sound advice regardless of vampires, in the event of finding oneself in a situation where a vampire might be nearby, carrying garlic, holy water, or a cross. Also, wear clothing covering the neck, arms, and legs. Finally, be aware of any strange behavior or people that may be encountered, and if feeling threatened, call

---

5   Barber, Paul (1988). Vampires, Burial and Death: Folklore and Reality. New York: Yale University Press.
6   Abbott, George (1903). Macedonian Folklore. Cambridge, University press.

for help immediately. Again, this is good advice regardless.

Are Vampires Real?

There are many people today that claim to be vampires. For those who choose to live as a vampire, the lifestyle transcends class, race, and gender. Thousands of people claim to be vampires and live a fitting lifestyle. So much so that there are Vampire Alliance organizations around the globe, these are safe places for those who choose to live as vampires. A place where they can be themselves and reveal their true natures. Some feel they need blood to survive others need human energy.

It is safe to say that at one point or another, almost everyone has had an encounter with an energy vampire. Within the vampire culture, this energy is necessary; without it, the vampire can suffer pain, depression, or illness.[7] Some vampires seek out the psychic energy present in crowds. However, there are those who live their lives as blood-sucking real-life vampires. Some have a group of people who offer themselves as nutrition.

Furthermore, the entire process is far more medical these days. Often medically trained personnel are present and handle the procedure for the donors and vampires. In this situation, a sharp implement is used to puncture the skin, and only a tiny amount of blood is consumed. The donors must complete the paperwork. No more attacks on the unsuspecting. Further, in today's world, donors must present certificates verifying that they do not have any blood-borne illnesses.

Do vampires really exist? In today's modern world, it is hard to believe that anything fantastical could possibly be real. But vampires have existed in cultures around the world throughout history. The term vampire is relatively new, yet stories of creatures with similar characteristics go back to at least 1500 BCE. The legend had to begin somewhere. So yes, in some form, vampires do exist today.

---

7   *A real vampire house*. Atlanta Vampire Alliance [AVA]. (n.d.). http://www.atlantavampirealliance.com/educational/vampirism.html

Chapter 2: Vampires of the Ancient World

Vampiric Origins
Today, vampires tend to be depicted as preternaturally beautiful creatures. In pop culture, vampires live in grand mansions, drive posh vehicles, and attend private schools for creatures of the night. But modern visions of vampires are based upon the vampire tales of the nineteenth century; specifically, Bram Stoker's Dracula. However, legends of vampires have existed for millennia. Various cultures throughout the ancient world had tales of unworldly spirits and blood-sucking entities considered precursors to modern vampires. Legends of the undead drinking the blood or eating the flesh of living beings are found in almost every culture around the world. Such stories have existed for many centuries.

The ancient world's vampires are considered creatures of the night that suck the blood of unsuspecting victims while they sleep. While the origins of these creatures remain a mystery, they have been found in many cultures throughout history. People of Ancient Greece and Rome believed that vampires were the undead. Furthermore, they believed that vampires could also be the spirits of those who had been wronged in life and who sought vengeance upon the living. Within Slavic mythology, vampires were demons that could be summoned to do their master's bidding. In some cases, the master could even control the vampire's behavior and use them as a weapon of sorts.

Various legends and folklore suggest that these creatures had the power to control the weather, create storms, and even cause disease. The vampire mythos also relates that they can shapeshift into animals or other creatures, such as bats or wolves. In some cultures, vampires could fly and change their appearance to that of a more attractive human form. Such mythology bears an important clue to early cultures and traditional beliefs. Water spirits reflect a dual nature of the ability to curse and bless. While the rains cause crops to grow, they can also destroy them, and early peoples rightly feared this reality. For example, believers in Aztec culture feared the water deity, Tlaloc, so worshippers appeased him through human sacrifice. Meanwhile, the ability to shapeshift resonates with humans' real fear of the face of wild animals such as wolves. He wandered closer to human settlements when winter made food sources lean for the wild wolf. The danger of becoming a food source for a hungry wolf was a legitimate reality. Vampiric lore reflects these fears, and blood is the central source of appeasement in all cases.

Traditionally, in most cases, the only way to protect oneself from these creatures was to wear items of garlic, holy symbols, and crosses. Descriptions of vampire attacks differ depending upon the region. In some circumstances, the victims were said to have been drained of their blood; in others, their heart was eaten, or their body was mutilated in some other way. For Centuries, vampires of the ancient world represented a source of fear, fascination, and mystery. While their exact origin remains a mystery, it is clear that many cultures throughout history feared and respected them.

Blood Cults of the Ancient World

Blood in the ancient world was magical. Viewed as the sacred life force of creation, it held a special place within the spiritual realm. While not specifically equated with the vampire, a general understanding of the significance of blood to the people of the ancient world sheds light on the beliefs about vampire-like creatures that evolved through time.

The practices of blood cults were observed throughout the world by numerous cultures. Many involved the ritual sacrifice of blood to honor and appease the gods. This blood typically came from either humans or animals and brought peace and prosperity to the people. In some cultures, animal blood symbolized fertility and its sacrifice brought fertility to the land. Consider the bull as a virile symbol, thus the blood of this animal would bring fertility to the land. Conversely, human blood was offered to show respect to the gods. For example, in the Maya culture, human blood must be offered to bring favor from the gods.

Additionally, blood cults brought protection from evil spirits. Remember, at this time the word for spirit was daemon or demon, and early peoples believed that illness and other calamities were caused by evil or angry spirits and gods. For the ancient Greeks and Romans blood sacrifice to the gods blocked any evil that may threaten their civilization.

In Ancient Egypt during the Old Kingdom Period (2700-2200 BCE), the deity Shezmu was worshipped.[8] The patron of ointment, perfume, and wine, he was also a god of blood. He possessed the ability to slaughter and dismember other gods. Scholars believe his worshippers used red wine to symbolize blood in religious offerings. One may also draw a parallel to the offering of wine as symbolic of the blood of Christ in Christian belief.

Honoring the dead was another purpose of blood cults. Mourners believed that the dead required blood to rest in peace. Within Egypt this practice was common. As mentioned previously, bulls were the animal sacrifice of choice in this ritual to appease the gods and ensure acceptance into the afterworld.

The importance of the blood cults of the ancient world cannot be overstated. They were a major part of religious and spiritual life in many ancient cultures. Such cults were used to bring good fortune, honor the gods, create social bonds, and as a form of justice.

The Goddess Sekhmet (1500 BCE Egypt)

The oldest vampire in the ancient world is Sekhmet. Sekhmet was a warrior goddess in ancient Egypt. Followers worshiped her as the goddess of war, healing, and destruction. Interestingly, many early deities of destruction also provided healing. Again, such themes are common in vampire legends. For example, small amounts of vampiric blood in the Anne

---

[8]   Pat Remler: Egyptian Mythology, A to Z. Chelsea House, New York 2010, ISBN 1438131801, p. 177-178.

Rice vampire universe offers healing for mortal ailments. A vampire may take life, yet also heal.

It was not unusual for artists to depict Sekhmet as a lion-headed woman. This description symbolizes her ferocity and strength. Physicians and healers credit her as their patron in her capacity as a healer.[9] To please her, worshippers would burn incense, leave food, and play music for her. Their prayers were whispered in the ears of cat mummies and given in offerings to her.

Sekhmet means she is powerful. She was revered as the sun god Ra's daughter and Ptah's consort. Legend states that Ra created Sekhmet from the fire of his eye as he gazed upon the earth. Created to protect him from his enemies and punish those threatening him. She was known for her fierceness and power and was said to be able to cause destruction with her fiery breath.

At the time, the term vampire did not exist, however, the description is synonymous. Sekhmet is described as a feline hybrid monster, whose tale historians consider the first story of an ancient vampire. In addition to being a warrior goddess, Sekhmet was also a goddess of death and healing. This combination of eternal death and eternal life simultaneously creates a sense of connection with vampire folklore.

In mythology, Sekhmet was said to have saved Egypt from destruction by destroying an army of evil spirits. She was also said to have been sent by Ra to punish the people of Egypt for their sins. Her father, Ra, saw man as unfaithful and disobedient. Therefore, Sekhmet was sent to slaughter humankind as punishment for their wicked ways. Sekhmet drank human blood as she killed people giving herself power.[10] To taper her bloodlust, Ra devised a trick. He dyed a massive

---

9   [9]*Sekhmet.* Explore Deities of Ancient Egypt. (n.d.). https://egyptianmuseum.org/deities-sekhmet#:~:text=Sekhmet%20was%20a%20terrifying%20goddess,a%20cure%20for%20every%20problem.

10   Lichtheim, Miriam (2006) [1976]. *Ancient Egyptian Literature, Volume Two: The New Kingdom.* University of California Press.

amount of beer blood red. Sekhmet drank it, thereby quelling her craving for blood. Despite her bloodlust being extinguished, her title in ancient Egyptian became translated to "Lady of Slaughter" as well as "One Before Whom Evil Trembles." Sekhmet remains an important figure in Egyptian mythology and is still worshipped by some today. Her image is seen in ancient Egyptian artifacts, and her power and influence are still remembered.

Empusa- Minion of Hecate (c 400 BCE Greece)

The Second oldest vampire in antiquity is Empusa or Empusai. They were fearsome daemons of the night. Empusa was the daughter of the goddess Hecate. Ancient documents describe her as a demonic, bronze-footed creature.[11] However, other legends claim that she has one leg made of bronze and the other was that of a donkey. Further, in some legends, her hair was made of fire. Empusa would transform into a beautiful young woman and seduce men as they slept. She would then attack and drink their blood.

Scholars claim that Empusa operated at the command of her mother Hecate. However, Hecate's precise nature is unclear. In modern times, worshippers view Hecate as being a queen of witches. According to the Byzantine Greek Lexicon, written by A.E. Sophocles in the 10th century CE, the Empusa was a companion of Hecate. The text is one of the few in existence that mention the Empusa in direct connection to the goddess Hecate. Due to Hecate's connection to magic, witchcraft, and the underworld, some scholars postulate that the Empusa was not a blood-related daughter of Hecate but an honorary one.

To be clear, during antiquity, daimones, or daemons, did not mean the same as now. Daemons were simply spirits. Hesiod recorded that the souls of men from the golden age were benevolent daimones on Earth. Therefore, daemons, or daimones, could be either fearsome or benevolent. These spirits of the ancient world could be protectors or bringers of

---

11 *An Intermediate Greek-English Lexicon*, Liddell, and Scott

catastrophe.

By late Antiquity, Empusa was regarded as a category of beings as opposed to a singular entity. Further, at that time, Empusa was no longer considered a daughter of Hecate, but rather a group of evil spirits controlled by her. The earliest references to Empusa come from the plays by Aristophanes. Empusa is traditionally viewed in conjunction with Lamia, Mormo, and Strix or Striges, all flesh-eating female demons in Greek folklore.

The Empousai and Lamia were the ancient equivalents of vampires and succubae--vampiric ghosts and demons. The Lamia is a mythical Greek and Roman mythology creature, typically represented as a half-woman, half-serpent. They are often described as having beautiful faces, long flowing hair, and a scaly lower body. Lamias are often portrayed as seductresses, luring men into their embrace and either draining them of their life force or devouring them. In some versions, they are also said to have wings and the ability to shape-shift. They are most commonly associated with the underworld and are sometimes thought to be the daughters of the goddess Hecate.

The Strix is a type of bird-like creature in Greek mythology. It is described as a large, owl-like bird of ill omen with a screeching voice. It is often associated with night and the unknown. In some accounts, the Strix is said to have been a fearsome harpy-like creature that haunted the night skies, attacking innocent people and animals. It was feared by the Greeks and was seen as a symbol of death and misfortune. In some cases, it was believed to be an agent of the gods, sent to punish mortals for their wrongdoings. Strix gave rise to the Transylvanian legend of the Strigoi, or vampire.

Lilith- Adam's First Wife (40 BCE, Israel)

According to ancient texts such as the Alphabet of Sirach (800 AD) and the Dead Sea Scrolls (40 BCE), Lilith was the first wife of biblical Adam, before Eve. Created at the same time as him and from the same mortal clay. Lilith refused to obey

Adam and was banished from the Garden of Eden.[12] Within Judaic lore, Lilith is mentioned as embodying various concepts and locals. Despite this, traditional rabbinic scholars tend to reject the existence of Lilith. Her legend grew during the Middle Ages with the rise of Jewish mysticism which may explain traditional scholars dismissed her existence.

According to folklore, Eve was created from Adam's rib after Lilith refused to be subservient. In Jewish Tradition, dating back 2,000 years ago or more, Lilith is a fascinating figure. The Hebrew term "lilit" translates to "Night creature" or "night monster." In Jewish folklore, she is a vampire-like child killer and the symbol of carnal lust. Ancient Jews believed in vampires, which they called "Lilith" or "Lilitu."

Lilith was believed to be a demon or female spirit who was cursed by God and sent to the underworld after refusing to obey Adam. The legend of Lilith states that she is a dangerous creature who preys on children and pregnant women, draining their blood and causing them to suffer from nightmares and other ailments. Many ancient Jewish texts, such as the Talmud and the Dead Sea Scrolls, describe Lilith as a vampire-like creature who feeds on the blood of the living. In some cultures, Lilith was believed to be the mother of all vampires and witches.

While Lilith has long been believed to be a hag or witch, she is now also a feminist icon. Further, Lilith has been depicted as the First Vampire in the *True Blood* television series. Additionally, Lilith's Jewish-American magazine regards her as an ancient, feisty, yet misunderstood woman. Her name derives from ancient Babylonian. It is a name for female demons and spirits. The ancient Babylonians believed that she recalled being human, so she crept into houses, killed wives, and took their place.

---

12   *Is menstruation a symbol of power or dangerous pollution?*. Blood, gender and power in Christianity and Judaism. (n.d.). https://www2.kenyon.edu/Depts/Religion/Projects/Reln91/Power/menspwr.htm

Ancient Babylonians believed vampires were demons of the dead who rose from the grave to feed on the living. According to Babylonian mythology, these demons had the power to possess the living and influence their behavior. They were thought to be able to transform into animals in order to gain access to the living. These vampires were believed to suck the life out of the living, causing them to become weak and ill. Ancient Babylonians believed these vampires could only be defeated by magical spells and charms.

Similarly, Jewish tradition speaks of Estries. These creatures are vampiric demon witches who prey on small children. However, they will consume an adult and their favorite is men. They are quite similar to the concept of a succubus. Estries have the ability to fly and change shape. Blood returns them to total health. Interestingly, the male counterpart to Estries is the werewolf, which displays characteristics similar to early vampire lore. Being seen or wounded by a human brings death to Estries.

Manananggal Demon of the Philippines (Before 900 CE)

The Manananggal is a mythical creature from Filipino folklore. Its name is derived from the Tagalog word tanggal which means to detach. A literal translation would be one that detaches. Additionally, the name also originates from an idiom used for a severed torso. However, there remain varying accounts of the features of a manananggal.

During the day, the creature appears as an ordinary human being. However, at night it transforms into a hideous beast. The Manananggal is typically depicted as a female monster or witch with the ability to separate her upper torso from her lower half at will. The upper half is able to fly off with huge bat-like wings and search for prey, usually in the form of unborn children or sleeping adults. Legend claims that the Manananggal favors preying on sleeping pregnant women. She uses an elongated antenna-like tongue to suck the hearts of fetuses or the blood of a sleeping person. It also haunts newlyweds or couples in love. Legend states that the

Manananggal was left at the altar; therefore, grooms-to-be are one of its primary targets.

The appearance of the Manananggal is often — if not always — accompanied by her birdlike companion, the Tiktik. This flying beast got its name from the sound that it makes: "tik-tik-tik-tik ". According to folklore, its presence is meant to confuse the unfortunate victims. The creature is commonly portrayed as being repelled by garlic, salt, and sharp weapons, just like traditional vampires. Further, people believe that spreading these items around a sleeping person can protect them from being attacked by a Manananggal.

Aswang of the Philippines

The Philippines has a unique belief in vampires, known as aswangs. An Aswang is a type of shapeshifting demon found in Philippine folklore. It is believed to be a man-eating creature that primarily feeds on the livers and hearts of its victims. It usually takes the form of a large black dog or a flying creature with the head of a pig and the body of a human. Aswangs are also said to be able to transform into other animals or objects and disappear into thin air. It is believed that Aswangs can be summoned by a spell or through a ritual and that they can be killed by stabbing with a special knife or being exposed to sunlight.

Often the Manananggal is confused with the Aswang. However, Aswangs are creatures that can shape-shift into animals such as dogs or birds as opposed to tearing themselves in two. The term Aswang has been used as an umbrella term for all sorts of ominous shapeshifting creatures in local folklore. One could argue that the Manananggal is a subspecies of the Aswang.

Although the creature has a long history in the realm of folklore passed down orally, the first written account dates to the 16th century. Spanish explorers in the Philippines created the first written record of the Aswang.[13] However, due to the

---

13   Prof. Geller, Sans' (2016, October 21). *Aswang - mythical creature*

geography of the Philippines, and the prevalence of oral tradition, the legend of the creature has evolved and been adapted depending upon the region.

Typically, the Aswang is said to have long fingernails and sharp teeth, and to feed on human organs, particularly the livers of unborn babies. They are believed to inhabit forests and cemeteries and can only be seen at night. Superstitions and protective rituals exist to ward off aswangs, such as placing thorns on doorways or performing a ritual in which a coconut is cut open and placed at a crossroads. It is believed that this will confuse the aswang and cause it to become lost.

There are theories as to the origins behind the folklore of this creature. First and foremost, is the natural call of nocturnal birds that have been mistaken for the sounds of the Aswang. Secondly, there exists a form of Parkinson's disease that primarily affects Filipino men. The afflicted often display symptoms such as uncontrollable muscle spasms, tremors, and contortions. Such behavior may have been mistaken for an Aswang transformation. Lastly, it is theorized that the Aswang legend explains disappearances and brutal murders in the area.[14]

Abhartach 5th Century

When one thinks of Ireland, fairies, leprechauns, and banshees may spring to mind. Celtic myths have greatly influenced modern pop culture. However, the vampire is the one icon rarely equated with Ireland. Interestingly, prevalent in Irish folklore exists vampires which possess no human heritage. Instead, they are a type of malevolent fairy. Abhartach is a vampire who has been a part of Irish folklore since the 5th century.

According to the author, Patrick Weston Joyce, Abhartach is another word for dwarf.[15] According to the book, 'The Origin

---

from Philippine. Mythology.net. https://mythology.net/monsters/aswang/

14   Prof. Geller, (2016, October 21). *Aswang - mythical creature from Philippine*. Mythology.net. https://mythology.net/monsters/aswang/
15   Joyce, P. W. (1910). The origin and history of Irish names of

and History of Irish Names of Places,' the dwarf was cruel and possessed powerful magic.[16] The locals feared him so much that a local chieftain killed him and buried him. To the horror of the townsfolk, the dwarf returned the following day and was eviler than before. The chieftain again killed him only to once again have Abhartach escape. This time he spread terror throughout Ireland.

The chieftain eventually succeeded in killing Abhartach a third time. However, he followed the advice of a Druid and buried the dwarf upside down which quenched the dwarf's magic, and he remained in his grave. This, however, is but one version of the legend.

In another legend, when Abhartach rose from his grave, he sought out fresh blood to drink. In this version, the chieftain seeks the advice of a Christian Saint who tells him to kill the dwarf with a wooden sword made from yew. Just as before, he was buried upside down, but this time a large stone was placed over the grave to lock him in.

In the form of a vampire, Abhartach is said to have been a merciless and cruel creature, feeding on the blood of his victims. He was also said to be able to transform himself into a wolf, bat, or creature of darkness. Upon leaving his presence, his victims would become weak, pale, and ill, and often die soon after. Abhartach is also said to have been able to hypnotize people, manipulate their minds, and even bring them back from the dead. He was a powerful creature, and many people still fear his name to this day.

---

places. Longmans, Green.
16   Ibid.

Chapter 3: Vampires of the Middle Ages

The belief in vampires during the Middle Ages (476-1599) was widespread and deeply rooted in popular culture. People believed that vampires were undead creatures that had risen from the grave and fed on the blood of the living in order to survive. This belief in the existence of vampires occurred for many reasons, including superstition, religious beliefs, and folklore.

In some parts of Europe, people believed that vampires were the result of a curse placed upon an individual. This curse was believed to be brought on by a variety of transgressions, from having committed a crime to being born with a deformity. In other parts of Europe, vampires were believed to be the result of a pact with the Devil or some other supernatural being. People also believed that magicians and sorcerers could summon and control vampires.

The fear of vampires was so strong that it led to the creation of preventative measures such as carrying garlic or holy symbols, placing crucifixes at the entrances of homes, and even the exhumation and burning of corpses suspected of vampirism. Although the belief in vampires during the Middle Ages was largely based on superstition and folklore, it still profoundly affected popular culture. Even today, the vampire myth still persists in many cultures.

The Plague

During the middle 14th century (1300's) the Black plague decimated Europe, the Middle East, and Africa. It claimed the lives of approximately 60% of the population. As one can imagine, such devastation changed the outlook and focus of society. Modern scientists exploring the Black Plague of the Middle Ages have traced its origins to Central Asia.

It erupted via trade ships transporting goods from the territories of the Golden Horde to the Black Sea.[17] Symptoms

---

17   [17] https://www.mpg.de/18778852/0607-evan-origins-of-the-black-

typically begin between one and four days after exposure. Infected present with headaches, fever, chills, weakness, and a watery or bloody cough. Bubonic plague leads to swollen lymph nodes of the neck which may spontaneously abscess and drain.[18]

Such symptoms may obviously point to a vampire. Bloody cough and swollen lymph nodes on the neck which may suddenly drain, to the superstitious mind, could reveal a vampire. Additionally, the practice of burying plague victims who had yet to expire and were coughing up blood existed. The supposed post-mortem activities of these undead victims fueled the vampire mythos. Commonly, gravediggers would bury corpses with a stone in their mouth to prevent future feasting on friends and neighbors.[19]

Vampire Graves

Modern archaeological excavations across Europe have revealed what scholars believe are vampire graves. Such burials were performed to prevent the deceased from rising out of their grave and wreaking havoc in the village. Practices and traditions varied from each locale.

It is not unusual for archaeologists to uncover burials in which skeletons are found with pieces of iron. This iron may have been nailed into the body of the deceased or placed on the body. Iron is said to repel vampires and evil spirits.

In Poland, numerous vampire graves have been excavated. The village of Starorypin Prywatny, located in the heart of Poland, was a bustling settlement during the Middle Ages. Excavations carried out by the Museum of the Dobrzyń Land of the area in 2008-2009 uncovered unusual burials. First, a burial

---

death-identified-150495

18   Vampires and the plague: Cause and effect? discuss. American Council on Science and Health. (2016, March 7). https://www.acsh.org/news/2015/10/30/vampires-and-the-plague-cause-and-effect-discuss
19   [19]Ibid

by the cemetery wall of a very tall man with several medical complaints. To be buried by the wall indicates a punishment as the deceased was abnormal. The skeleton revealed that the man had severe crowding of his front teeth and other physical defects that would have ostracized him from others. Other misfit graves of the region included a man buried face down with his hands tied behind his back, a woman with a padlock near her shin to prevent her from rising from the dead, and a woman whose head had been removed.[20]

One of the reasons that Middle Europe has so many deviant graves is their folk beliefs. Drunks, murderers, and thieves according to Slavic folklore are the most likely to become vampires. Additionally, those who were not baptized, drowned, or committed suicide were likely candidates for vampirism. While the term vampire was not coined yet, these beings were undead revenants who fed on human blood. As such, they became blamed for a wide variety of ailments including the plague.[21]

The graves of purported blood-drinking undead creatures exhibit curious rituals every day to supposed vampire graves. By placing a brick in the mouth of the deceased, the undead remained unable to feed and prey on the living. Folklore relates to pinning or staking a suspected vampire to their grave to prevent resurrection. Furthermore, during the Middle Ages standard practices included burying the deceased face down, decapitation, or stuffing the mouth with garlic. Whether such tactics proved helpful is subject to speculation. However, the fact that modern archaeologists are uncovering such burials points to the use of practices of keeping vampires in their

---

20   Rich, V. G. (2022, May 29). Strange burials reveal fear of vampires in Old Poland. or do they?. Haaretz.com. https://www.haaretz.com/archaeology/2022-05-29/ty-article-magazine/strange-burials-reveal-fear-of-vampires-in-old-poland-or-do-they/00000181-0f3c-d1d5-afd5-8f7edc140000
21   [21]Barrowclough D.Time to Slay Vampire Burials? The Archaeological and Historical Evidence for Vampires in Europe. Firstpublished:19.10.2014. Cambridge: Red Dagger Press

graves.

Vlad the Impaler (1431-1476)

Vlad III was a 15th-century ruler of Wallachia, now part of Romania, known for his cruelty and popularly believed to be a vampire. He is often associated with the vampire legend due to his cruel and unusual methods of punishing his enemies. He was known for impaling his victims on stakes, which earned him the nickname "Vlad the Impaler."

Vlad III, Vlad □epe□ or Vlad Dracula, was the second son of Vlad Dracul (Vlad the Dragon), the former ruler of Wallachia.[22] As a young man in 1442 Vlad Dracula was held, along with his younger brother, by the Ottoman Empire as a hostage to secure the loyalty of the elder Vlad.[23] In 1447, the elder Vlad was murdered by Hunyadi, the Hungarian regent-governor, when Wallachia was invaded. Vlad's cousin was appointed as a military leader, or overlord, for Hungary and the following year they invaded the Ottoman Empire.

This history is important in understanding the actions which earned Vlad Dracula his moniker of Vlad the Impaler. With the help of the Ottoman Empire, Dracula entered Wallachia illegally. However, upon his cousin's return, Dracula returned to the Ottoman Empire. The relationship between his cousin and Hungary deteriorated over the course of the next 5-6 years thus allowing Dracula to invade Wallachia with Hungarian support to reclaim his rightful place.

To send a very clear message, a purge of the Wallachian nobility was undertaken by Dracula to strengthen his position. Further, the German settlers who supported his enemies were targeted. Their villages were razed and plundered. Those captured were taken to Wallachia and impaled. The actions of Vlad Dracula, while cruel and barbaric, brought peace to the

---

22 [22] The name Dracula is a nickname and is loosely translated to mean the son of the dragon. However, in modern Romanian, Dracul means devil, thus contributing to Dracula's reputation.
23 Treptow, Kurt W. (2000). *Vlad III Dracula: The Life and Times of the Historical Dracula*. The Center of Romanian Studies.

region in 1460.

As a vampire, Vlad the Impaler is depicted as a powerful, ruthless ruler who was capable of terrorizing his enemies. He is often depicted as bloodthirsty and cruel, with a penchant for torture and violence. For example, an incident from history shares close ties with a piece of vampiric folklore. A vampire may not enter a home unless invited. While pursuing a thief who had tried to hide in Dracula's home, a group of soldiers burst in without invitation or warning. As a result, Vlad ordered the commander to be executed for entering his premises without invitation.[24]

Vlad Dracula was imprisoned, exiled, and even reviled for his barbaric actions throughout his life and reign. As such a polarizing figure it is rational that stories of his antics abound. However, these stories must be taken with a dose of skepticism as many are a combination of fact and fiction.[25] For example, many of the stories equate his life to a vampire, such as the rumor that he was seen dining in a field of soldiers he has just killed and dipping his bread in their blood.

Vlad the Impaler was known for his appetite for human flesh. According to some legends, he would impale his victims and then feast upon their blood. In some folk tales, he is said to have drained the blood of his victims, giving him a sinister, vampiric appearance. He was believed to be able to transform into a large black bat or a wolf, granting him supernatural powers that he used to his advantage. However, these attributes came about after Stoker's novel *Dracula*.

Vlad the Impaler is an iconic figure in vampire lore and history. His legend has been the inspiration for countless works

---

24   Hasan, Mihai Florin (2013). "Aspecte ale rela☐iilor matrimoniale munteano-maghiare din secolele XIV–XV [Aspects of the Hungarian-Wallachian matrimonial relations of the fourteenth and fifteenth centuries]". Revista Bistri☐ei (in Romanian). XXVII: 128–159.
25   McNally, Raymond T. (1991). "Vlad ☐epe☐ in Romanian folklore". In Treptow, Kurt W. (ed.). *Dracula: Essays on the Life and Times of Vlad ☐epe☐*. East European Monographs, Distributed by Columbia University Press. pp. 197–228.

of fiction and film. He is often seen as a symbol of evil and darkness, but also a reminder of the lengths humans can go to achieve their goals.

Countess Bathory (1560-1614)

Female serial killers are a rarity. As a matter of fact, according to experts, less than 20% of serial killers are women.[26] Also known as the Blood Countess, Elizabeth Bathory is one of the most prolific female serial killers to date. Elizabeth Bathory, a Hungarian noblewoman, was accused of torturing and killing over 600 young women, between 1590 and 1610, mainly in Transylvania.[27] Further, she was said to have bathed in the blood of her victims to remain eternally youthful. She is listed in the Guinness Book of World Records as the biggest serial killer of all time.

Her legend has been passed down from generation to generation, However, modern scholars question if she committed the crimes levied against her. It is agreed that she was gorgeous but prone to fits of anger from an early age. As a noblewoman, her marriage strengthened an alliance between Transylvania and Hungary. When her husband died in battle, she inherited his property. Fully adept at handling an estate, she ran hers well until she was imprisoned in 1610 for murdering noblewomen, beatings, and torture. They tried to add in the charge of witchcraft. All charges she denied.

According to folklore, however, Countess Bathory is a legendary vampire. She was an aristocrat and a noblewoman who became known for her dark and mysterious ways. The legend of Countess Bathory is that she was a beautiful vampire. She was said to have been married to a wealthy noble person. Some legends report that due to her vampiric nature, she could

---

26   Sussex Publishers. (n.d.). Female serial killers. Psychology Today. https://www.psychologytoday.com/us/blog/the-human-equation/201205/female-serial-killers
27   Ramsland, Katherine. "Lady of Blood: Countess Bathory". Crime Library. Turner Entertainment Networks Inc. Archived from the original on 11 March 2014.

not bear any children while others claim she bore illegitimate children while her husband was away at war.

Legend relates that she began to feast on the blood of others. She was said to have held nightly feasts in which she invited local villagers and drank their blood. This behavior soon caused suspicion and fear in the local townspeople, and it is said that she was eventually caught and put on trial for her crimes. The countess was found guilty and sentenced to death. However, it is said that before her death, she cast a powerful spell that cursed the city of Vác so that any vampire who entered the city would be destroyed.

To this day, the legend of Countess Bathory is still told in the city of Vác, and it is said that her curse still remains. Many believe that her vampiric nature caused her to become the vicious creature she was and that her curse still protects the city from other vampires. Conversely, historians argue that the charges against her were a political ploy designed to destroy the power and influence of the Bathorys.

Gilles de Rais (1404-1440)

Gilles de Rais, a 15th-century French nobleman, has been the subject of many a vampire tale. His story is complex, with his life being one of fame and tragedy. Born in 1404, de Rais was a brave and valiant soldier, and one of the most prominent knights of his time. He fought alongside Joan of Arc in many battles and was even granted a position in the court of Charles VII. However, de Rais' life was not all glory and high honors. This French nobleman was accused of killing hundreds of children and was believed to have been a vampire.

By the 1430s de Rais became accused of dabbling in the occult sciences. During his trial in 1438, Eustache Blanchet, a priest, states that de Rais petitioned him to find those able to summon demons and practice alchemy. During this time period, Europe experienced a rise in the practice of magic. This took many forms from alchemy to medicinal folk magic, to darker occult studies. Additionally, this is the time period in which the prosecution of witches began to increase. While men were also convicted of witchcraft, they were often executed on other charges such as murder.[28]

Despite his interest in the occult, de Rais's attempts to summon a demon were fruitless.[29] De Rais stood trial accused of murdering and sacrificing children in satanic rituals. Trial transcripts are heart-wrenching and gruesome.[30] De Rais was a sadistic monster who took a perverse delight in the torture and murder of innocents. While the actual number of victims is unknown, rumor places the total between 100-200. Gilles de Rais confessed to his crimes in a court of law on October 21, 1440.

His death sentence was carried out on October 26th, 1440. There are several legends about de Rais, claiming that he was an undead creature of the night, drinking the blood of the living in order to survive. In some versions of the tale, he is even said to have been seen in the area of his castle, taking the form of a bat-like creature. His victims harken back to early vampire-like creatures of folklore that prey upon infants and children.

Legend relates that he also ate his victims. Despite the stories and legends, no concrete evidence exists of de Rais' vampiric nature. His life, however, does make for an interesting and compelling tale. Whether de Rais was an actual vampire, he will forever remain one of the most fascinating figures of the Medieval period.

Revenants

Are the above examples vampires? Or are they unstable murderers? Maybe even political victims. In the 12th century, historians Walter Map and William of Newburgh wrote about

---

28   APPS, LARA, and ANDREW GOW. "INVISIBLE MEN: THE HISTORIAN AND THE MALE WITCH." In *Male Witches in Early Modern Europe*, 25–42. Manchester University Press, 2003. http://www.jstor.org/stable/j.ctt155j84b.6.
29   Bataille, G., Rais, G. de, & Robinson, R. (2004). The trial of Gilles de Rais: Documents. Amok.
30   Benedetti, Jean (1971), *Gilles de Rais*, New York: Stein and Day, p113.

accounts of revenants.[31] According to folklore, a revenant is an animated corpse that has been revived after death and haunts the living.[32]

In William of Newburgh's *Historia*, he recounts several cases of vampire-like revenants. For example, a man who had died was given a Christian burial. However, he rose from his grave at night and began to wander through the town. He attempted to return home where he crawled into bed with his widow. He did this three nights in a row and then began to harass his brothers. He returned to his widow and brothers night after night, but companions watched over them. Soon all the houses in the village kept watching for him. Eventually, the townspeople called upon the bishop. The grave was opened, and a letter of absolution was placed upon the chest of the man. He then remained in his grave.[33]

The above story shows that a revenant is commonly used interchangeably with the word vampire. William of Newburgh wrote,

"It would not be easy to believe that the corpses of the dead should sally (I know not by what agency) from their graves and should wander about to the terror or destruction of the living, and again return to the tomb, which of its own accord spontaneously opened to receive them, did not frequent examples, occurring in our own times, suffice to establish this fact, to the truth of which there is abundant testimony."

He did not discount the stories of such creatures out of hand. For Medieval society, such a scenario appeared perfectly possible. As remarked earlier in this chapter, the decimation of the plague that first lasted between 1347-1351 changed how

---

31   William of Newburgh; Paul Halsall (2000). "Book 5, Chapter 22–24". Historia rerum Anglicarum. Fordham University
32   Carl Lindahl; John McNamara; John Lindow (2000). Medieval Folklore: A Guide to Myths, Legends, Tales, Beliefs, and Customs. Oxford University Press.
33   [33] William of Newburgh: book five. Internet History Sourcebooks: Medieval Sourcebook. (n.d.). https://sourcebooks.fordham.edu/basis/williamofnewburgh-five.asp#22

society viewed death and the afterlife. Further, the plague recurred numerous times between 1361-1400. People had a front-row seat to death. Entire families and whole communities were completely wiped out.

Psychologically, society was preoccupied with death causing them to turn toward mysticism, magic, and the occult. It is entirely plausible that revenants did rise from the grave. History is full of examples of premature burials. Add to this the two best-selling books of the era, the Malleus Maleficarum[34] and the King James Bible. Citizens wanted a reason for the death, a person, or an evil devil to blame.

The Middle Ages set the stage for the Victorian fascination with all things supernatural. It prepared the world for monsters that are still popular today. And it gave rise to the most famous of them all.

Count Dracula.

---

[34] The Hammer of the Witches written by Sprenger and Kramer. A treatise on malevolent witchcraft.

Chapter 4: The Victorian Vampire

Contrary to Medieval vampires who were equated with revenants and serial killers, the Victorian Vampire took on a new symbolism. The concept of vampires has evolved throughout history, and Medieval and Victorian vampires are two distinct representations of this creature. Here are some comparisons and contrasts between the two:

1. Origin: The medieval vampire is deeply rooted in Slavic folklore (Which will be discussed in the following chapter) and was believed to be a corpse that rose from the grave to feed on the blood of the living. On the other hand, the Victorian vampire was popularized in Victorian literature and was often portrayed as aristocratic and seductive.

2. Appearance: The medieval vampire was typically depicted as a gruesome, decomposing corpse with long fangs and bloodshot eyes. The Victorian vampire was often portrayed as an attractive and alluring figure, with pale skin, sharp features, and elegant clothing.

3. Powers: The medieval vampire was often seen as a powerful and supernatural being, with the ability to transform into an animal, control the weather, and cause disease. On the other hand, the Victorian vampire was typically portrayed as having more subtle powers, such as mind control and shapeshifting.

4. Symbolism: The medieval vampire was often associated with evil, disease, and death, and was feared by the people. The Victorian vampire, however, was often seen as a symbol of forbidden desire and sexual taboo and was often romanticized in literature.

5. Cultural influence: The medieval vampire significantly impacted Slavic folklore and has continued to be a popular figure in Eastern European culture. The Victorian vampire, however, has had a much broader cultural impact, with countless books, films, and TV shows featuring this creature.

While Medieval and Victorian vampires represent the same blood-sucking creature, they differ in origin, appearance, powers, symbolism, and cultural influence. Further, real-life incidents involving serial killers and cannibals fueled the flames of vampire legends in the Medieval era while the Victorian Vampire became a literary construct.

Those Crazy Victorians!

The Victorian era (1820-1914) was a time of great fascination with the supernatural. With the rise of Gothic literature, the idea of vampires began to gain a foothold in the public imagination. During the Victorian era, vampires were seen as creatures of the night, dark and mysterious, and often associated with the aristocracy. Vampires were thought to be undead creatures, no longer living, but still possessing a form of existence.

In the Victorian era, vampires were believed to be creatures of the night, who emerged from their coffins to feed on the blood of the living. They were thought to have an insatiable thirst for blood and were often described as having an inhuman strength and a hypnotic power over the living. In addition to having the ability to shape-shift and turn into bats, vampires were also believed to have the power to mesmerize their victims into submission.

Victorian vampires were often portrayed as seductive and glamorous figures. They were regularly described as being dressed in luxurious clothing and had a certain charm about them. It was also believed that vampires had the power to mesmerize their victims, making them fall under their spell and become victims of their vampiric desires.

The Victorian era saw the emergence of a number of vampire-related stories, novels, and plays. Bram Stoker's novel, Dracula, was one of the most influential works of the time and helped to popularize the idea of vampires in the public imagination.

Vampires during the Victorian era were often seen as symbols of death and destruction and were often used to represent the dark and mysterious forces of the supernatural. Despite this negative connotation, vampires still retained a certain degree of fascination and allure. Even today, vampires continue to captivate audiences and remain a popular subject in literature and film.

The Victorian fascination with vampires was rooted in a combination of scientific advancements, superstition, and literature. During this period, people were fascinated with the idea of a creature that was both dead and alive at the same time, as medical science began to advance and allow people to view the dead body in a new way. At the same time, superstitious beliefs surrounding the undead were still strong, especially as it related to Mesmerism and the occult. Finally, the popularity of the Gothic novel and the works of authors such as Bram Stoker and Mary Shelley helped to fuel the fascination with vampires during this era.

Dracula, published in 1897, gave us the template for the modern vampire. He took Transylvanian folklore and spun it in a way that would influence the vampire legend for over a hundred years. Dracula cemented vampire weaknesses such as garlic, sunlight, and crosses. Yet, one of the most lasting myths is the inability of the vampire to view his reflection in a mirror. It is a symbolic representation of their lack of a soul, as they are not truly alive. It could also be linked to their immortality, as they are physically unchanging and therefore cannot recognize their own reflection. Fun fact: in the 1800s silver was used as backing for mirrors, thus creating a reflection. As silver is one of the purest metals that repels vampires, it would have been logical that mirrors would not reflect a vampire at the time. But beware, modern mirrors are backed with aluminium, and vampires can now be seen in mirrors!

Changing Victorian Roles

The social landscape during the Victorian Era was shifting and Victorian writers used the archetype of the vampire to indicate this. Such novels reflected the social landscape and through this, writers expressed criticism of issues permeating Victorian society. For example, issues such as drugs, religion, and science were accurate representations of society within gothic vampire stories.

Victorian society was a class-based hierarchy with wealthy

white men at the top of the pyramid. Britain was the most powerful empire in the world at this time, but this does not mean that the everyday citizen was satisfied with the status quo. Socially, a gender gap existed, to put things politely. Gender ideology during this time was introduced on the doctrine of separate spheres. In short, men and women were different and therefore meant to do different things. For example, men were strong while women were weak. Sex was central for men while reproduction was the greatest aim of women. Further, men exuded independence while women required a man on which to lean. As such, men belonged in the public sphere, while women belonged in the unseen private sphere.

If such ideologies were not enough, add in ethnicity and the social gap widens. In response to this, the Victorian vampire became a protest against the socio-cultural environment of the period.[35] Further represented are the conflicts of old over new. As the age of reason dominated Europe, traditionalists pushed back, thus paving the wave for gothic fiction.

Carmilla

The 19th century was full of gothic horror. Newspapers and literary magazines first published gothic stories in the form of regular serials. Gothic horror is characterized by a setting that creates fear in the reader. They feature threats of the supernatural and blending the past with the present as old secrets come to the surface.[36] This aspect of the present being haunted by the past sets gothic fiction apart from other genres. For example, featuring a dark and foreboding old castle. Such is

---

35 [35] t, P. by. (2022, March 3). "From the Victorian Vampire to the Contemporary Vampire" by Horace Tam. Department of English, Hong Kong Baptist University.
https://buhk.me/2018/11/20/vampires/#:~:text=From%20The%20Vampyre%2C%20Carmilla%20to,criticise%20issues%20pervading%20Victorian%20society.
36 [36] Hogle, Jerrold E., ed. (29 August 2002). "Introduction". The Cambridge Companion to Gothic Fiction. Cambridge Companions to Literature (1 ed.). Cambridge University Press. pp. 1–20.

the case in the story of *Carmilla*.

Written in 1872 by Joseph Sheridan Le Fanu, Carmilla is a sinister and seductive creature who feeds on the life force of humans, usually in the form of their blood.[37] The story is told from the point of view of the character Dr. Hesselius, the first literary occult detective. Interestingly, the author departs from the typical Victorian themes regarding women as helpless creatures without a man. On the contrary, In *Carmilla*, the men are the helpless ones.[38]

Carmilla is a powerful vampire, capable of shapeshifting, teleportation, and other supernatural abilities. She is also immortal and can drink the blood of her victims to sustain her strength. In addition, she has the ability to mesmerize her victims, making them susceptible to her will. Carmilla is a classic example of a vampire that has been around for centuries and continues to cause fear and terror in those who cross her path. However, during this period, the female empowerment within the story caused greater fear. So contrary to Victorian female norms, this brazenness created fear in the hearts of men.

Her pale skin and dark eyes lend her an ethereal beauty, and her long dark hair frames her face in a mysterious manner. Carmilla is a particularly dangerous vampire, as she is known to use her powers of seduction and manipulation to lure unsuspecting victims into her clutches, primarily women. She is known to leave a trail of destruction in her wake, leaving death and ruin behind her.

Interestingly, real-life events inspired this story. A priest had investigated a town three years earlier. Allegedly, a vampire had been terrorizing the townsfolk. Coming from the cemetery, a vampire entered the homes of townspeople and terrorized them in their beds. A Hungarian traveler came to the village and upon learning of their trouble decapitated the vampire in

---

37   The Project Gutenberg eBook of Carmilla, by Joseph Sheridan Le Fanu. (n.d.). https://www.gutenberg.org/files/10007/10007-h/10007-h.htm
38   Veeder, William. "Carmilla: The Arts of Repression." *Texas Studies in Literature and Language* 22, no. 2 (1980): 197–223. http://www.jstor.org/stable/40754606.

the cemetery thus freeing the town. This story became incorporated into the thirteenth chapter of the *Carmilla* story.[39] Additionally, some elements came directly from the 1751 dissertation by Dom Augustin Calmet, a French Benedictine monk. He wrote about magic, vampires, and the apparitions of spirits from Hungary, Moravia, et al. Additionally, the legends of Elizabeth Bathory from the previous chapter played a role in shaping the character of Carmilla.

Varney the Vampire

Varney the Vampire, or the Feast of Blood, is a 19th-century gothic novel by James Malcolm Rymer and Thomas Peckett Prest. First published in 1845, it is considered to be one of the earliest works of vampire fiction. Further, it introduces many of the images present in subsequent vampire novels and stories. For example, this is the first reference to a vampire possessing fangs. "With a plunge, he seizes her neck in his fang-like teeth."[40]

The novel follows the story of Sir Francis Varney, a mysterious and seemingly immortal vampire who terrorizes the English countryside. Varney's victims include the Bannerworth family, who are at first unable to identify the source of their suffering. Once a wealthy household, they were driven to economic collapse when their father died. Such backgrounds reflect the struggle between tradition and modernity.

Despite the efforts of the family and their friends to protect them, Varney continues his reign of terror. In the course of the novel, Varney's background is slowly revealed, as is the source of his immortality. The novel is notable for its vivid descriptions of horror and the supernatural and its sly wit. The narrative also provides an early example of the vampire genre, which would later become popularized in books such as Dracula. Varney's influence can still be felt in modern literature

---

39   LeFanu, J. Sheridan (2016). *Carmilla: Annotated with Notes.* pp. 114–115, 146–147.
40   Prest Thomas Peckett James Malcolm Rymer and Devendra P Varma. 1970. *Varney the Vampire; or the Feast of Blood: The First in a Series of Gothic Novels.* New York: Arno Press.

and cinema, as it has inspired numerous books, films, and TV shows. Most recently, Varney was featured in the 2018 film What We Do in the Shadows, where he was featured as an old vampire who still lives in the shadows. Varney the Vampire remains a horror genre classic, and its influence can still be felt in modern works.

Lord Ruthven

Lord Ruthven is an iconic vampire who originated in the horror novel The Vampyre by John William Polidori in 1819. He is said to be the progenitor of all modern vampires and is often depicted in literature, films, and television. Further, Lord Ruthven is considered the origin of romantic vampire fantasy fiction. This story began as part of the story told by Lord Byron during a contest with Polidori, Mary, and Percy Shelley. This same contest brought about the novel Frankenstein by Mary Shelley.[41]

Lord Byron's Fragment of a Novel is an unfinished vampire horror story. The main character is Augustus Darvell. However, Lord Ruthven is modeled on Lord Byron himself. Polidori traveled with Lord Byron as his personal physician. When *The New Monthly Magazine* published *The Vampyre*, they erroneously attributed the story to Lord Byron. Both men wrote letters to correct the error. Polidori remarks that while Lord Byron did the groundwork, it was he who developed the story.[42]

Polidori presents Ruthven as a powerful and seductive creature with a sinister presence. He is symbolic of the fear of a corrupt aristocracy that permeated Victorian society. Ruthven is a gentleman and blends in with society. Earlier vampire novels described them as revenants or undead corpses. The idea of something so sinister hiding in plain sight provides fodder for

---

41   The Preface to the 1818 edition of Frankenstein written by Percy Bysshe Shelley. Shelley stated that three participated in the ghost-writing contest. Mary Shelley stated that four participated in the contest in the 1831 Introduction, adding herself to the contest and leaving out Claire Clairmont.
42   Beresford, Matthew (2008). From Demons to Dracula: The Creation of the Modern Vampire Myth. London: Reaktion Books

real fears of the time. Further, the story revolves around the victim, Aubrey, an aristocratic young man.

Ruthven is described as having a pale complexion, dark eyes, and a cold and calculating demeanor. His physical appearance often changes from one form to another, allowing him to blend in with his victims. He is also a master of disguise, able to take on the form of a wolf, bat, or other animals.

In spite of the deadly hue of his face, which never gained a warmer tint, either from the blush of modesty or from the strong emotion of passion, though its form and outline were beautiful, many of the female hunters after notoriety attempted to win his attentions and gain, at least, some marks of what they might term affection.[43]

Lord Ruthven is immortal and can only be killed by a stake through the heart or exposure to sunlight. He has an insatiable hunger for human blood and often goes on night-time hunts to feed his cravings. His victims are usually beautiful young women, whom he seduces and manipulates into giving him their blood.

He has an alluring and mysterious charm that is irresistible to those he encounters. Lord Ruthven is one of the most iconic vampires of all time. His cunning and manipulative nature has earned him a place in popular culture and made him a symbol of fear and horror.

Count Dracula

A chapter on the Victorian vampire is only complete with discussing Count Dracula. This literary icon is the basis for much of the vampire lore today. He has influenced pop culture in a way that no other has. Count Dracula is a legendary vampire, based on the character in Bram Stoker's 1897 novel, *Dracula*. At this time scientific discovery, trade expansion, and industrialization were at their height. Like other literary vampires of the time, he represents the fear of societal progress

---

[43] John Polidori, ""The Vampyre"," The Vampyre, Lit2Go Edition, (1819), https://etc.usf.edu/lit2go/96/the-vampyre/1654/the-vampyre/.

in the Victorian era.

He is a centuries-old Transylvanian vampire and the main antagonist of the novel. The novel tells the story of Dracula's attempt to move from Transylvania to England in order to find new blood and spread his evil influence. Within this time period, the blood represents sexual immorality within the context of the novel. Further, he is from Transylvania; for Victorian Europe, that area was considered part of Eastern culture. The uncertainty of the unknown exotic East struck fear in the hearts of readers.[44]

Count Dracula is often portrayed as a commanding, powerful, and seductive figure. He is usually described as tall and pale, with a long cape and a pair of piercing eyes. Typically seen as an embodiment of evil, his monstrous nature is used to frighten and repel people. He is a potent symbol of the supernatural and continues to fascinate and terrify readers and viewers alike. Count Dracula remains a timeless character that is most closely associated with Victorian-era England. He represents the dark and mysterious forces of the supernatural, and his presence in literature and film remains a reflection of Victorian society's fascination with the occult.

Again, the Victorian era was a time of great social, political, and scientific advancement, and the literature of the period often reflected the changing times. Count Dracula is a perfect example of this, as he embodies the fears and anxieties of the period. The Victorians were preoccupied with death and the afterlife, and Dracula is a reminder of the dangers of the unknown. He also serves as a metaphor for the fear of outsiders and the spread of disease and a warning against the dangers of power and control.

The Gothic themes of the Victorian era are also reflected in the character of Count Dracula. He is both repulsive and

---

44   Hollingsworth, A. (2019, January 9). Fear of Progress: Medium. https://medium.com/@lexiloulee/fear-of-progress-b42fc00c023a#:~:text=Dracula%20represents%20the%20Victorian%20fear,the%20anxieties%20of%20our%20time.

alluring at the same time, and his dark and mysterious nature speaks to the Victorian fascination with the supernatural. His powers of seduction and manipulation reflect the Victorians' fear of the power of the wealthy and powerful, while his immortality symbolizes the fear of death and the unknown. Count Dracula is a classic example of the Victorian era's fascination with the supernatural and the power of fear. He is a symbol of the fear of the unknown, a reminder of the dangers of power and control, and a warning against the spread of disease. He is an enduring character that continues to fascinate audiences today.

Chapter 5: Slavic Vampires

Within the context of vampire folklore, it is important to examine cultures and regions of the world separately. The previous chapters outline the evolution of the vampire from its earliest incarnation into the literary creature of the Victorian Era. Further, the legend of Vlad ☐epe☐, a historical Romanian figure, while lending his name to the iconic figure of Dracula, shared little else with the character.

Bram Stoker originally dubbed his antagonist Count Wampyr. He knew little of the historical ruler Vlad Dracula, or Vlad ☐epe☐. According to historian Elizabeth Miller, Stoker used miscellaneous scraps of Romanian history and the name of Dracula. Further, Mr. Stoker's notes bear no mention of Vlad ☐epe☐, or Dracula.[45] With such information, what then is the reality of the Slavic vampire?

Slavic Death Beliefs

Common Slavic belief indicates a stark distinction between soul and body. The soul is not considered to be perishable. The Slavs believed that upon death the soul would go out of the body and wander about its neighborhood and workplace for 40 days before moving on to an eternal afterlife. Thus pagan Slavs considered it necessary to leave a window or door open in the house for the soul to pass through at its leisure. During this time the soul was believed to have the capability of re-entering the corpse of the deceased. Much like the spirits mentioned earlier, the passing soul could either bless or wreak havoc on its family and neighbors during its 40 days of passing.

Upon an individual's death, much stress was placed on proper burial rites to ensure the soul's purity and peace as it separated from the body. The death of an unbaptized child, a violent or untimely death, or the death of a grievous sinner (such as a sorcerer or murderer) were all grounds for a soul to become unclean after death. A soul could also be unclean if its body

---

45   Miller, E. R. (2005). A Dracula Handbook. Xlibris.

was not properly buried. Alternatively, a body not given a proper burial could be susceptible to possession by other unclean souls and spirits. Slavs feared unclean souls because of their potential for taking vengeance.[46]

Some of the more common causes of vampirism in Slavic folklore include being a magician or an immoral person; suffering an "unnatural" or untimely death such as suicide; excommunication; improper burial rituals; an animal jumping or a bird flying over the corpse or the empty grave (in Serbian folk belief); and even being born with a caul. [47] Slavic vampires were able to appear as butterflies, echoing an earlier belief that the butterfly symbolized a departed soul.[48]

Among the beliefs of the East Slavs, those of the northern regions (i.e. most of Russia) are unique in that their undead, while having many of the features of the vampires of other Slavic peoples, do not drink blood and do not bear a name derived from the common Slavic root for "vampire". Ukrainian and Belarusian legends are more "conventional". However, in Ukraine, vampires may sometimes not be described as dead or seen as engaging in vampirism long before death. Ukrainian folklore also described vampires as having red faces and tiny tails.[49]

Romanian Vampires

Romanian Vampires have a long and varied history. Romanian vampires were known as moroi (from the Romanian word mort meaning 'dead' or the Slavic word meaning

---

46 Perkowski, J. L. (1976). Vampires of the Slavs. Slavica Publishers Inc. pp. 21–25.
47 Burkhardt, "Vampirglaube und Vampirsage", p. 225
48 Kanitz, Felix (1875). *Donaubulgarien und der Balkan: Historisch-geographische Reisestudien aus den Jahren 1860-1878* (in German). Leipzig: Hermann Fries. pp. vol. 1 (1875), p. 80.
49 Kubijovyč, V., Struk, D. H., & Zhukovsky, A. (1985). Encyclopedia of Ukraine. Publ. for the Canadian Institute of Ukrainian Studies, the Shevchenko Scientific Society (Sarcelles, France), and the Canadian Foundation for Ukrainian Studies by University of Toronto Press.

'nightmare') and strigoi, with the latter classified as either living or dead. Live strigoi were described as living witches with two hearts or souls, sometimes both.[50] Strigoi were said to have the ability to send out their souls at night to meet with other strigoi and consume the blood of livestock and neighbours. Similarly, dead strigoi were described as reanimated corpses that sucked blood and attacked their living family. Live strigoi became revenants after their death, but there were also many other ways for a person to become a vampire.

  The earliest known reference to a vampire in Romania dates back to the 11th century when a monk named Eraclius wrote about an undead creature that could be found in the Carpathian Mountains. This creature was called a strigoi, which is the Romanian word for vampire. Strigoi is a type of undead vampire-like creature in Eastern European folklore. They are said to be the reanimated corpses of people who had died with unfinished business or had been cursed by a witch. Strigoi are typically described as having pale skin, long claws, red eyes, and a preference for drinking human blood. They are usually depicted as being able to shapeshift and are said to be able to fly. Strigoi are said to be able to create familiars to do their bidding, and they can influence people's thoughts and dreams. Strigoi are typically seen as malevolent and dangerous creatures, and they are often used in stories to create fear and dread.

  During the 18th century, Romania was under the rule of the Ottoman Empire. During this time, there were numerous reports of vampires roaming the countryside. Vampires in Romania in the 18th century were believed to be the reanimated corpses of people who had died prematurely, usually due to a violent death or suicide. They were believed to leave their graves at night and feed on the blood of the living, usually targeting family members. People believed vampires could be identified by their bloated corpses and long, sharp nails. To protect themselves

---

50   Cremene, A., & Zemmal, F. (1981). La Mythologie du vampire en Roumanie. Editions du Rocher. p. 89.

from vampires, people would place garlic, iron, and holy objects around their homes or the graves of their loved ones. To destroy a vampire, people would often stake them or decapitate them. These reports were taken so seriously that the local people took measures to protect themselves from these creatures. This included placing garlic and crosses around the house and using holy water to drive away the undead.

During the 19th century, the vampire was a popular figure in Romanian literature and folklore. The vampire was depicted as a creature of seduction and a monster to be feared.

Vampires in Romania in the 19th century were believed to be the undead, the reanimated corpses of people who had died. They were believed to come out at night and drink the blood of their victims, usually by biting them. Vampires were thought to be able to transform into animals, and some were said to have the ability to fly. Belief in vampires was widespread, with peasants often exhuming the bodies of suspected vampires and driving a stake through their hearts in order to prevent them from rising again. Vampires were also believed to be able to cause illness, crop failure, and other misfortunes. As this belief in vampires was so widespread, some superstitious practices were developed in order to ward off vampires, such as placing garlic or wolfsbane around homes and carrying wooden crosses, holy water, and other religious artifacts.

Popular literature of the time also portrayed the vampire as a noble figure, a symbol of Romania's struggle against foreign rule. Today, the vampire still exists in Romanian folklore and is still believed by some to be a real creature. Modern vampires in Romania are often portrayed as creatures of the night, who are believed to feed on the blood of their victims in order to survive. They are often seen as seductive, mysterious, and powerful, with an alluring and dangerous air about them. They have been portrayed in folk tales and horror stories, as well as in films and books. They are typically seen as living in dark and foreboding castles and forests and having superhuman strength and abilities. They are also said to shape-shift into other creatures and have hypnotic powers. Although the vampire is no longer feared in the same way it once was, it still remains an important part of Romania's culture and history.

Russia

Russia is now the most powerful Slavic country. It is a nation rich in folkloric history and includes legends of vampires. The vampires in Russian folklore share similarities with those of other Slavic nations. However, unlike the concept of a single vampire-type creature, Russian folklore has several legends of different types of vampires.

The Slavic vampire myth goes back to pre-Orthodox folk belief. It serves as an explanation of death and the physical personification of the tragedies experienced by the community. The vampire's symbol personified tragic events and established a useful system of imagery. This imagery exceeded its folkloric beginnings entering the realm of Russian literature. It became a steady literary device from the eighteenth century to post-Soviet fiction.[51]

The Upyr

The Upyr is one of the most famous Russian vampire legends and is the primary vampire species. Unlike other vampires in popular culture, the Upyr is not believed to be undead, but rather a living creature with supernatural powers. Legends of this creature vary from region to region; therefore, characteristics alter depending upon the source. The origins of the Upyr vampire legend are unclear, but it is believed to have originated in Eastern Europe, particularly in Russia and Ukraine. In Russian folklore, the Upyr is often associated with witches and sorcery and is said to be able to summon other supernatural creatures to do its bidding.

Primarily, it is said that this creature was once a living person

---

51 [51] Townsend, Dorian Aleksandra, From Upyr' to Vampire: The Slavic Vampire Myth in Russian Literature, https://unsworks.unsw.edu.au/entities/publication/80028c0b-77ad-4250-a037-ea95a082b44a

who made a pact with the devil to gain immortality and supernatural powers. It is described as having pale skin, long black hair, pointed ears, and sharp teeth. Further, they are often described as having tweo hearts and two souls.[52] The Upyr is said to feed on the blood of its victims, turning them into vampires themselves.

In the 19th century, the Upyr legend gained widespread popularity in literature and art. Famous Russian authors such as Nikolai Gogol and Aleksey Tolstoy wrote stories featuring Upyrs, and artists such as Viktor Vasnetsov created vivid and eerie paintings of the creature. AK Tolstoy penned his short story *Upyr* in 1841. It details the story of a family cursed with vampirism due to the woman of the house being unfaithful.

Croatia, Slovenia, the Czech Republic, and Slovakia

In Croatia, Slovenia, the Czech Republic, and Slovakia, a type of vampire called pijavica, which literally translates to 'leech', or 'drinker' is used to describe a vampire who has led an evil and sinful life as a human and in turn, becomes a powerfully robust and cold-blooded killer.

Incest, especially between mother and son, is one of the ways in which a pijavica can be created. Then it usually comes back to victimize its former family, who can only protect their homes by placing mashed garlic and wine at their windows and thresholds to keep it from entering. It can only be killed by fire while awake and by using the Rite of Exorcism if found in its grave during the day.[53]

Prague, the Czech Republic's capital, is the country's largest city. It was home to the Bohemians for more than 1,000 years. Stories of magic, alchemy, and hermetic teachings have been told for centuries. Prague blends the cultures of Central Europe, Slav, and the Jewish. As a medieval town, citizens

---

52   [52] Oskar Kolberg (1874). *Lud: jego zwyczaje, sposób...* Vol. t. VII - Krakowskie, cz. 3.
53   *Vampire Universe: The Dark World of Supernatural Beings That Haunt Us, Hunt Us, and Hunger for Us*, Jonathon Maberry. Kensington Publishing Corp: New York, 2006. p 16-17

simultaneously maintained a religious fervor while embracing superstitions of the supernatural. Czech archaeologists discovered compelling data that during the shift between Paganism and Christianity, the belief in vampires was prevalent throughout the Czech region.

In 1966, archaeologist, Jaroslav Špaček, visited a town near Prague called Čelákovice. There, he unearthed skeletons dating to the 10th century which had been determined to be "improper" burials. Such burials indicated vampiric burials. For example, some remains were bound by hand and foot, others were decapitated, and some were buried face down. This turned out to be the largest vampire graveyard found. Further, it is the only burial ground reserved specifically for the burial of suspected vampires.[54]

Professor Giuseppe Maiello of Charles University in Prague, specializing in folklore, examined the findings. He remarks that the belief in vampires was so common in Eastern Europe that citizens during the 10th century, even though in the 17th century, firmly believed that vampires were real. As such, the above-mentioned graves were true "vampire burials."

The Great Vampire Epidemic

Physicians began investigating cases of vampirism during the 1730's. Travelers through Eastern Europe since the late 1600s noted in their journals vampiric events. Doctors reported physical symptoms of a vampire attack as shivering, spasms, nausea, nightmares, and even death. In 1732, seventeen articles published in professional journals reported the vampire epidemic. This was followed by twenty-two treatises relating to vampirism.

Austrian authorities dispatched to Slavic territories to investigate the Vampire Epidemic and wrote reports detailing strange phenomena that could not be explained. These reports

---

54   [54] thelastromantik_. (1970, January 1). Vampires in Eastern Europe. https://elltimoromntico.blogspot.com/2014/12/vampires-in-eastern-europe.html

revealed that Slavic villagers were being preyed upon by vampires.[55] Further, the prey soon became vampires as well. According to reports, they were mindless monsters who craved blood.

Modern scholars point to a misunderstanding of disease, decomposition, and sheer fearful superstition as the leading cause of the panic and belief in a Vampire Epidemic. Additionally, one must recognize the historical events in the area during this time. Between imperial wars and treaties causing the Ottoman Empire to surrender much of its Eastern territory to the Austrian Hapsburg monarchy, the Slavic countries were in considerable unrest.

Former Slavic territories rested along the Southern Borderlands of the new Hapsburg Empire. The outbreak began in the village of Medveda. While not the first to experience revenants or vampires, it was here that the outbreak of mania began. From October through November 1731, a series of unexplained deaths occurred in the village. This sparked an investigation by the military as the village was under the mercenary rule of the Hapsburg Empire. Suspecting an epidemic, the commander, Lieutenant-Colonel Schnezzer organized a quarantine commission and set off for the village.

Epidemics were not unusual at the time. However, the fact that the village rested at the intersection of two major trade routes complicated the situation. The doctor attached to the commission determined that the sick were afflicted with religious pre-Christmas fasting undertaken by the villagers. However, the villagers claimed vampirism.

According to the locals, they knew exactly who caused the affliction and told the following story.

"There used to be two women in the village who during their lifetime became vampirized (haben sich vervampyret), and it is said that after their death they will also become vampires and will vampirize (vervampyren) yet others."[56]

---

55   Dundes, A. (2006). The vampire: A casebook. The University of Wisconsin Press.

To satisfy the villagers, the doctor agreed to exhume the bodies of the deceased and was shocked at what he found. Some were in natural states of decay while others appeared fresh. He attempted to come up with a reasonable explanation scientifically, yet he was left empty-handed. As a result, he refused to offer a concrete diagnosis. However, he did adopt local vernacular in his reports and used the words vampyer and vervampyren.[57] This marked the first time vampirism was used in a medical report.

---

56   ÖStA FHKA AHK HF "Vampir Akten – ☐eil 2," 1134v
57   [57] Ádám Mézes, **Vampire Contagion as a Forensic Fact** The Vampires of Medveđa in 1732, Historical Studies on Central Europe 1.1, 149–176, Apr 30, 2021
         https://www.academia.edu/48972393/Vampire_Contagion_as_a_Forensic_Fact_The_Vampires_of_Medve%C4%91a_in_1732

Chapter 6 Asian Vampires

The Asian concept of the vampire is generally more closely related to myths and folklore than the traditional Western concept of the vampire. Unlike Western vampires, Asian vampires are often more closely related to ghosts and are not necessarily associated with drinking blood. In many Asian cultures, vampires are believed to be undead spirits that haunt the living, causing harm and death. They are also believed to take different forms, such as a bat, cats, fox, and other animals. Additionally, Asian vampires are often associated with a specific location or object and can only be destroyed by destroying the source of their power.

The Penanggalan

The Penanggalan is an ancient creature from Southeast Asian folklore that has been a source of fear and fascination for centuries. This creature is described as a female vampire which typically appears as an invisible disembodied head with entrails attached. During the night, the Penanggalan will detach its head from its body and fly through the air, seeking out its victims to feed on their blood.[58] The Penanggalan was believed to have been created when a woman broke a powerful tabu or committed a heinous crime such as murder or adultery. Such actions would draw the ire of the gods and they would curse the woman to become a Penanggalan. It was also believed that a Penanggalan could be created if a pregnant woman ate a certain type of fruit that a shaman had cursed.

The Penanggalan would typically feed on infants, pregnant women, and the elderly, as they were believed to have the most vital essence.[59] It was also believed that the Penanggalan could be repelled by particular objects such as garlic, mirrors, and holy symbols. In modern times, the Penanggalan has become more of a cultural icon than a source of fear. The creature is

---

58   Regan, S. (2019). The vampire book. Dorling Kindersley Limited.
59   Griffiths, K. (2016). Vampires. Cavendish Square Publishing.

often featured in movies and television shows, often portrayed as a dark and mysterious figure. Despite this, the Penanggalan remains a powerful symbol of fear and caution for those who live in Southeast Asia. This vampire-witch hybrid is said to be an old woman by day and a flying disembodied head with entrails dangling below at night. The Penanggalan is said to roam the streets, attracted to the sound of babies crying in search of their next meal.

The Krasue

The Krasue is a terrifying vampire-like spirit from Southeast Asian folklore. It is said to be the spirit of a deceased woman or young girl who is cursed to wander the night in search of human blood. Typically, this creature is the spirit of a woman who died in childbirth. She has a beautiful female face and a long tongue that can reach up to 30 feet in length. Further, the Krasue is believed to wander the streets at night in search of its next victim.[60] Similar to the Penanggalan, she is described as having a floating head with an entrails-like body trailing behind her and is said to have a burning hunger for human flesh.

True to vampiric folklore, the Krasue is most active during the night and can often be seen hovering near human settlements, searching for victims. It is said that the Krasue is attracted to the scent of human blood and will hunt down anyone who is bleeding or injured.[61] She will use her long entrails-like body to wrap around her victim and slowly drain them of their life force. When the Krasue is not hunting for victims, she is said to haunt the homes of those who have wronged her or her family. She will often appear in the form of a female ghost and will haunt the house until she is appeased with offerings of food and

---

60   Ancuta, K. (2017). Beyond the Vampire: Revamping Thai Monsters for the Urban Age. ETropic: Electronic Journal of Studies in the Tropics, 16(1). https://doi.org/10.25120/etropic.16.1.2017.3564
61   Lundberg, A., & Geerlings, L. (2017). Tropical Liminal: Urban Vampires & Other Blood-Sucking Monstrosities. ETropic: Electronic Journal of Studies in the Tropics, 16(1). https://doi.org/10.25120/etropic.16.1.2017.3574

incense.

The Krasue is a powerful and dangerous spirit. According to legend, those who encounter her should take all necessary precautions. It is said that the best way to ward off a Krasue attack is to burn incense and recite prayers to the spirit. Some also recommend wearing protective amulets or talismans to ward off the spirit's hunger. Although the Krasue is a terrifying spirit, she is also seen as a symbol of justice. It is said that the Krasue will seek out those who have wronged her and that she will consume their life force in order to restore balance to the world. Such beliefs harken back to the sacred and feared goddess archetype. As stated previously in this book, early vampires were women, and in many areas of the world, these mythological blood-sucking creatures remain in the realm of feminist social beliefs. Such beliefs have roots in pre-colonialism before female subjugation. As with other areas of the world, Asian vampire legends reflect social norms and taboos.

Japan

The Japanese vampire, or Kyūketsuki, has been a part of Japanese culture for centuries.[62] In Japan, vampires are not usually depicted as human-like creatures with long, sharp fangs and white skin. They are known to feed on human life force and are believed to be spirits, gods, or other supernatural beings. Interestingly, early Japanese society did not fear the idea of a blood-sucking undead. Only after Feudal Japan was opened to the wider world did such creatures become something to fear.

The Japanese vampire has been featured in a variety of popular works of fiction, such as films and manga. In traditional Japanese folklore, vampiric-type entities were often believed to be the spirits of people who had died in a cruel or dishonorable manner and were cursed to haunt the living as undead monsters. However, Western imaginings have changed

---

62   Multiple translation communities in Contemporary Japan. (2017). ROUTLEDGE.

this representation.[63]

There are a variety of different types of vampires in Japan, including the Yuki-onna, a female vampire who appears in a white kimono; the Karasu-tengu, a crow-like vampire; and the Nurarihyon, a shape-shifting vampire.[64] It is believed that these creatures, being in the spiritual or supernatural realm, are impervious to the weapons traditionally used against the Western vampire.

Despite their fearsome reputation, vampires in Japan are often portrayed as humorous and playful characters rather than as monsters. In some cases, vampires can even be seen as helpful and friendly companions. While the Japanese vampire may not be as famous as it once was, it still remains a popular part of Japanese culture and is still seen in popular works of fiction. Whether you find them fascinating or frightening, the Japanese vampire is sure to leave an impression.

Yuki-onna

The Yuki-Onna, or Snow Woman, is a powerful spirit of winter and snow, hailing from Japanese folklore.[65] Her legend dates back to the Muromachi Period (1336-1573), and her story was told by the poet Sōgi. While her legend does not fit the traditional stereotype of the vampire, there are several attributes which reflect similarly to the vampire mythos.

There are several variations of the Yuki-Onna legend across Japan. According to legends from Niigata Prefecture, A stunningly beautiful woman came to visit a man and, of her own volition, became his wife. However, she was reluctant to enter the bath, and when forced to do so, she vanished into thin

---

63   Morita, N. (2020). Japan beyond its borders: Transnational Approaches to film and Media. Seibunsha.
64   Sari, Ida A. L. "The Figures and Meanings of Tengu: Semiotic Study of Mythological Creatures in Japanese Folklore." Humanus: Jurnal Ilmiah Ilmu-ilmu Humaniora, vol. 19, no. 2, 2020, pp. 217-229, doi:10.24036/humanus.v19i2.109943.
65   [65] Bane, Theresa (2012). Encyclopedia of Demons in the World Religions and Cultures. McFarland & Company. p. 334.

air, leaving behind only thin, fragmented, floating icicles. Each region possesses its own version of the Yuki-Onna legend. However, there remain common threads across the regions.

On a snowy night, Yuki-onna appears as a tall and beautiful woman with long black hair and blue lips. Her skin is so pale it almost looks transparent, allowing her to blend into the snowy landscape - as famously described in Lafcadio Hearn's Kwaidan: Stories and Studies of Strange Things. She is often seen wearing a white kimono, but some legends describe her as being nude, with only her face and hair standing out against the snow.[66] Despite her captivating beauty, her eyes can fill mortals with terror. She moves gracefully across the snow, leaving no footprints - some tales even say she has no feet! If threatened, she can transform into a cloud of mist or snow. Truly a mysterious and enchanting figure!

The Yuki-Onna is a fearsome spirit and is said to cause great suffering to anyone who crosses her path. In some regions, she is known as a snow vampire wandering the snowy lands during winter, searching for humans to prey upon. If she finds someone, she will freeze them with her icy breath and then consume their life force. It is said that she can even turn humans into the snow after she has killed them. Her appearance also resembles the iconic vampire visage in that she is very pale yet stunningly beautiful at the same time.

Despite her fearsome reputation, the Yuki-Onna remains a captivating creature. While not all stories portray her in a positive light, she is still an important figure in Japanese folklore and a reminder to be careful in the winter months.

Karasu-tengu

The Karasu-tengu are a unique breed of tengu, a long-nosed supernatural creature found in Japanese folklore. Tengu are a type of mischievous supernatural beings.[67] The Karasu-tengu

---

66   Seki, Seigo Seki (1963), Folktales of Japan, p. 81, University of Chicago
67   [67]Bellingham, David; Whittaker, Clio; Grant, John (1992). Myths

are usually depicted as having a large, curved beak, long, pointy ears, and long red noses. Traditionally, they resemble the crow or raven, yet, like the vampire, they have also been depicted as posing doglike features. The Karasu-tengu are known for their mischievous behavior, often playing tricks on humans and other creatures. They are said to live in forests and mountains and, like vampires, have the ability to fly through the air. Some stories say they can even transform into humans and birds, just as the classic vampire can transform into a bat or canine.

Karasu-tengu are powerful creatures and can be dangerous if provoked. It is said that they are able to manipulate the weather, cause natural disasters, and even bring curses upon those who anger them. Throughout history, the infamous Karasu-tengu has been associated with mysterious Buddhist and yamabushi practices, as well as the mysterious kami-kakushi phenomenon, where a person (usually a child) is mysteriously abducted for days or weeks. Kami-Kashi is the term used to describe a mysterious disappearance or death of a person. Typically, that person was said to have angered the gods, or kami.[68] Again, while not vampiric in the traditional sense, the Karasu-tengu characteristic of causing villagers to disappear, often returning with memory loss, or mysteriously dying, is reflected in the traditional tales of vampires who abduct mortals and hold them prisoners, such as Count Dracula and Mr. Renfield.

Through time, this being has undergone a transformation. For example, like the traditional Western version of the vampire, the Karasu-tengu possesses the ability to shapeshift. While the Western vampire represents an antithesis to Christianity, as in the cross and Holy water repels him, the Karasu-tengu is the Eastern dispute against Buddhism. Many of the stories have altered over time in response to the spread of Buddhism to

---

and Legends. Secaucus, New Jersey: Wellfleet Press. p. 199.
68   [68]Reider, Noriko T. (April 2005). "Spirited Away: Film of the Fantastic and Evolving Japanese Folk Symbols". Film Criticism. 23 (3): 4–27, 79.

frighten followers away. Regardless, the Karasu-tengu remains a popular figure in Japanese culture today. They are often featured in anime and manga series and in various video games. Additionally, they are popular in other pop culture realms, appearing in various films, television shows, and books.

Nurarihyon

The legend of the Nurarihyon, an ancient and powerful yokai, dates back centuries in Japan. Yokai are a class of supernatural entities and spirits in Japanese folklore. The word yōkai is composed of two kanji characters which both mean "suspicious, doubtful."[69] The Nurarihyon is a powerful and peculiar figure that is said to be the leader of all yokai. He is a supernatural being who is said to have the ability to control the weather, the cycle of nature, and even the fate of mankind. The Nurarihyon is a slippery creature that is rarely seen and even more rarely caught. He is often described as a tall, dark figure with a long, white beard and a pointed head. In truth, his appearance more closely resembles the modern concept of a grey alien than that of a vampire. However, like the modern vampire, he is said to travel in the shadows, often using the darkness to his advantage. I one legend it is written, "While night is still approaching, the nurarihyon comes to visit as the chief monster."[70] Many believe that the Nurarihyon is the source of all evil in the world and, like other vampire myths around the world, is responsible for spreading disease, famine, and suffering.

The legend of the Nurarihyon has been passed down for generations, and his power and influence have been the subject of many stories and myths. He is said to be able to summon and control powerful spirits and demons, and to be able to grant wishes and make deals with humans. He is also said to be able to see into the future and find out secrets that no one else

---

69 Foster, Michael Dylan (2009). Pandemonium and Parade: Japanese Monsters and the Culture of Yōkai. University of California Press.
70 Eihiko Fujisawa "Complete Works of Yokai Gadan: Japan", Chuo Bijutsusha, 1929, page 291

knows. The Nurarihyon has many names depending on the region, but he is most commonly known as the Lord of the Yokai. No matter what name he is given, it is clear that the Nurarihyon is a powerful and mysterious figure that still has a strong presence in Japan today.

India

India has several links to the modern vampire, owing to its vast mythology and folklore. Some scholars believe that vampire mythology actually began in India and spread throughout Eastern Europe to Greece and back along the spice and silk trails.[71] It may not be the traditional image of a vampire that comes to mind. However, there are some creatures in Indian folklore that could be considered more vampire-like than the vampire itself. The most commonly known form of the vampire in Indian folklore is the vetala, an undead being that inhabits cemeteries, ruins, and other dark places. It is said that the vetala feeds on the blood of humans or animals and has the ability to take on different forms. Furthermore, it is believed to possess supernatural powers, such as the capacity to fly and the ability to cause disease. In addition to the vetala, Indian folklore also mentions other vampire-like creatures, such as the brahmaparush and the kalivarush. The brahmaparush is a vampire-like creature that feeds on the souls of the dead and can take the form of a cat or a dog. The kalivarush is said to be a vampire-like creature which resides in the jungles and can take the form of a human. Indian beliefs about vampires also include the belief that certain rituals or powerful curses can create vampires. These vampires are said to be extremely powerful, able to control the elements and manipulate the minds of their victims. Despite the prevalence of vampire beliefs in India, there is no evidence to suggest that these creatures actually exist. However, some people still believe in

---

71   Gupta, D. (2022). Vampires -A study on Vampires in Indian folklores by Debajyoti Gupta. Supernatural Studies and Other Social Issues Book .

the existence of vampires and continue practicing rituals and other superstitious beliefs to protect themselves from these creatures.

Vetala

It is believed that most of the knowledge Indians possess regarding Vetala is derived from the stories of Vikram and Betaal of Betaal Pachisi, which were written in the 11th century. However, Vetala has a much more profound and unsettling history. According to mythology, Vetala is said to possess corpses in cemeteries and haunt the nearby villages and their inhabitants. It has been observed that certain spirits utilize reanimated corpses as a means of transportation. It has been further noted that a vetala has the capacity to possess and subsequently depart from a deceased body at their own discretion.[72] Such abilities harken to the early vampire beliefs of revenants.

It is further believed that Vetala is responsible for a variety of horrific occurrences, such as the murder of children and miscarriages. It is thought that they are caught in a state known as 'the twilight zone,' which lies between life and the afterlife.[73] Interestingly, are temples in honor of Betal in various regions. Betel is a deity in charge of beings such as ghouls and vampires. Neither entirely dead nor entirely alive, Vetala certainly bears a resemblance to the vampires of modern times.

The Rakshasa

The Rakshasa is a humanoid creature from Hindu mythology. The female is known as Rakshasi, and regardless of gender, the name means man-eater.[74] Legend relates that they are a

---

72   Dowson, John (2013-11-05). A Classical Dictionary of Hindu Mythology and Religion, Geography, History and Literature. Routledge. p. 355.
73   Rosen, Brenda (2009). The mythical creatures bible : the definitive guide to legendary beings. New York: Sterling. p. 193.
74   [74]Rakshasas. Vyasa Mahabharata. (n.d.). https://www.vyasaonline.com/encyclopedia/rakshasas/

powerful and mysterious race of creatures that inhabited the many realms of ancient India. They were often portrayed as shape-shifting demons who had the ability to take on forms of animals, humans, and even gods. The Rakshasa is said to have been created by the breath of Brahma, the creator, while he was sleeping after Satya Yuga, or the first of the four Yugas.

Following their creation, they were filled with bloodlust and began to feed upon Brahma himself! In response, Brahma shouted, "Rakshama!" This is the Sanskrit word for "Protect me!" The god Vishnu came to his rescue and banished the Rakshasas to earth. First attested to in the Vedic sources of Hymn 87 of the tenth mandala of the Rigveda, they are classified with the Yatudhana:the beings who consume raw flesh.[75]

The Rakshasa was said to have a variety of powers, including shapeshifting, invisibility, and the ability to fly. Further, similar to the common vision of the vampire, they possess two fangs extending from the top of their mouths. They can smell human flesh and have an insatiable appetite. They were also known to possess superhuman strength and powerful magical abilities. Rakshasa were widely feared across India, as they were known to be vicious, cruel, and dangerous. They were often seen as omens of bad luck and danger and were thought capable of bringing misfortune and destruction to those who crossed their path.

The Rakshasa were also known to be great warriors and often used as soldiers in the armies of gods and kings. They were said to be fierce fighters and could even be summoned to fight in the battle for their masters. Today, the Rakshasa are still revered in many parts of India, and their legends and stories are still told and celebrated in Hindu culture. This creature is said to be a demonic being that takes the form of a human during the day and a creature of the night at night. The Rakshasa is said to feed on the blood of its victims, and its presence can cause sickness

---

75 [75]Rig Veda. The rig veda in Sanskrit: Rig veda book 10: Hymn 10. (n.d.). https://sacred-texts.com/hin/rvsan/rv10010.htm

and death.

The Churel

Originating in Persia, the Churel was said to be the spirits of women who died with "grossly unsatified desires."[76] However, the Churel in India is believed to be the spirit of a woman who died while pregnant or during menstruation.[77] Such beliefs harken back to early depictions of vampire-like creatures as female. Further, it is a reminder of the various spiritual and cultural beliefs surrounding blood and femininity. As such, the Churel is considered the ghost of an unpurified living thing.[78]

Similar to early vampire creatures around the globe, the Churel is normally depicted as a female figure with the lower body of an animal. She is said to be able to shape-shift into a variety of forms, such as a peacock, owl, or mongoose. However, she the form of a beautiful woman in order to seduce young men. She will lure them into the woods or mountains, where, instead of feeding on blood, she feeds on their life force. Further, rather than kill them, it turns them into old men.

However, according to lore, there are exceptions to this tendency. If the Churel perished due to mistreatment from the family members, she would avenge her death by attacking the men of the family. She begins with the youngest male and drains him of blood until he becomes a shriveled-up old man. Interestingly, the victims become old rather than die. Though, once done with the males of the family, she moves on to others and if one should harken her call, he may die. [79]

The Churel is a feared creature in many parts of India, and it

---

76   DeCaroli, Robert (2000). "Reading Bhājā: A Non-Narrative Interpretation of the Vihāra 19 Reliefs". East and West. 50 (1/4): 271
77   [77]Leshnik, Lorenz S. (1967). "Archaeological Interpretation of Burials in the Light of Central Indian Ethnography". Zeitschrift für Ethnologie. 92 (1): 23–32.
78   Crooke, William (1894). An Introduction to the Popular Religion and Folklore of Northern India. p. 69
79   Crooke, William (1894). An Introduction to the Popular Religion and Folklore of Northern India. p. 69

is believed that the only way to ward off its evil influence is to perform special rituals. Like other cultures, when a woman dies a traumatic or otherwise tragic death, a family may bury her in a manner to prevent her from returning as a Churel. The Churel is an important part of Indian folklore and is a symbol of the fear and superstition that many people in rural India still feel towards the supernatural. In modern times, the Churel has become a popular subject in books, films, and television shows, and its dark reputation continues to terrify and fascinate people around the world.[80]

Pishachas

Vampires can be compared to a class of blood-sucking Pishachas. Within Dharmic religions, Pishachas are flesh-eating demons. They are considered the very manifestation of evil. [81]Their description might be a bit different from the traditional vampire, but the class of beings called Pishachas, are very similar. There are mentions of various types of Pishachas in many ancient books.

Like the Rakashasas, the Pishachas were also created by Brahma, according to one legend. However, according to another, they were the sons of Krodha (anger). Folklore describes them as having red, bulging eyes such as those of modern vampires. Pishachas are nocturnal and hunt cremation grounds during the night. They are also believed to have the power of shapeshifting and becoming invisible. Like other vampiric creatures from this area of the world, they feed upon human energy. What we, today, would call an energy vampire. Apparently, they could also possess humans and drive them insane.

With sunlight as an opposing force, the Pishacha is close to your standard vampire in many ways – darkness-loving, blood-

---

[80] "Haunted Tales: In Conversation with 'Dhaka Paranormal Society". Daily Sun

[81] "Thakumar Jhuli" ঠাকুরমার ঝুলি (PDF). bdnews24.com (in Bengali). Archived from the original (PDF) on 2016-03-07.

hungry, and carrying the overall appearance of a vampire doppelganger.[82] Unlike other vampire legends, the Pishacha is a race separate from humans. A human cannot become a Pishcacha. Indian flesh-eating demons, though different from the modern concept of the vampire, bear striking similarities to the lore and perhaps played a role in creating and spreading the legend. Who knew that India had a part to play in this, too?

Legend of the Asian Vampire

Vampires are a classic figure in many cultures around the world, and Asian vampire folklore is no exception. From China to India, Japan, and beyond, these creatures of the night have been featured in stories and legends for centuries. In China, vampire-like creatures were known as "Jiang Shi" or "Hopping Vampires."[83] They were said to be corpses brought back to life by a sorcerer and were characterized by their greenish complexion and ability to hop and fly. Legends of these creatures often featured them terrorizing villages, drinking the blood of victims, and kidnapping children.

In India, the vampire was known as the "Bhuta," a malevolent spirit that inhabited the bodies of the dead. They were said to cause misfortune, illness, and even death. Powerful magicians and priests could only stop these creatures. In Japan, the vampire was known as the "Kyuuketsuki," a creature that could turn into a bat and often fed on the blood of humans. These creatures were also said to have the power to take on human form and control the minds of their victims.

In Thailand, the vampire was known as the "Phi Tai Hong," a creature with a human body and the head of a buffalo. These creatures were believed to cause sickness, bad luck, and death to those they encountered. Finally, in Korea, the vampire was

---

82   Mani, V. (1975). Purānic encyclopaedia purānanighaṇṭu, Engl. A comprehensive DICTIONŔY with special reference to the epic and purāịc literature.
83   Lam, Stephanie (2009). "Hop on Pop: Jiangshi Films in a Transnational Context". CineAction (78): 46–51.

known as the "Gumiho," a creature that could transform into a fox or a beautiful woman and had the power to seduce humans. They were said to feed on the flesh and blood of humans and were also believed to possess magical powers.

No matter where you look in Asia, you can find stories and legends of vampires that have been passed down through the generations. These creatures have terrorized and fascinated people for centuries and continue to do so today.

Chapter 7: Vampires of Africa and the Middle East

The Western concept of vampires has been romanticized and popularized through books, movies, and television, while the African concept of vampires is much more rooted in mythology and folklore. The Western concept of vampires is of an undead creature, usually human in form, craving human blood. They are generally seen as immortal, powerful, and seductive. They are often portrayed as villains, but sometimes as the hero or anti-heroes. They often have superhuman strength and supernatural powers, such as the ability to turn into a bat or a mist. In some stories, they can hypnotize their victims and control their minds.

In contrast, the African concept of vampires is much more diverse and complex. Vampires in African folklore are seen as supernatural beings with various powers, ranging from shapeshifting to controlling the weather. They can also be seen as a force for good or evil. For example, some African cultures view vampires as protectors of their homes, while others view them as a source of danger and chaos. Vampires in African folklore also have a variety of origins. Some are born, others are created by a witch doctor or sorcerer, while others are formed from the spirits of the dead. They are often associated with death and destruction and are seen as a source of fear and dread.

The Western and African concepts of vampires are quite different, yet they both have a long and fascinating history. By understanding them both, we can gain insight into how different cultures interpret the mysterious and powerful creatures of the night.

Adze

The people of Togo and Ghana tell the story of the Adze. It is a vampiric being in Ewe folklore.[84] The Ewe people, living

---

84   Bunson, Matthew (1993). *The Vampire Encyclopedia*. London: Thames & Hudson Ltd. p. 2.

along the coastal regions of West Africa, are an ethnic group of Ghana. The Ewe people share the common linguistic culture of Gbe, a cluster of approximately twenty similar languages spoken between Ghana and Nigeria. According to Ewe folklore, when in the wilds, the Adze takes the form of a firefly. However, it transforms into a human shape upon capture. While in human form, the adze has the power to possess humans.

Those possessed by an Adze are considered witches. In many African communities, the belief in witchcraft is deeply rooted. In Ghana, for example, this belief continues to shape everyday life. Traditional African spiritual beliefs depict the universe as being made up of a multitude of spirts which may be called upon to inflict evil or good on mortals.[85] Such beliefs in Ghana can be traced back for hundreds of years, well before colonial powers entered the country. Witches are set apart from healers in that their magic is used for evil, while a healer's magic is used for good.[86] Within the context of the Adze, witchcraft is referred to as "spirits" who have lost their status as humans due to an interaction with harmful spirits.

This form of vampire differs from the common Euro-centric vampire model. However, it more closely resembles the modern concept of a psychic or energy vampire. For example, the Adze's influence would negatively affect the people who lived around its host. There are perceived signs that a person is possessed. For example, women with brothers whose children fared better than their own, old people who survived when young people started dying, and the poor if they envied the rich. An Adze would feed on the energy of another causing difficulties in the victim's life. In such situations, and with the required caveats, the Adze's effects are generally felt by the possessed victim's family or those of whom the victim is

---

85   Benyah, Francis (2017). "Equally able, differently looking: discrimination and physical violence against persons with albinism in Ghana". Journal for the Study of Religion. 30 (1): 161–188.
86   [86]Roxburgh, Shelagh (31 December 2016). "Witchcraft and Violence in Ghana". Cahiers d'études africaines (224): 891–914. doi:10.4000/etudesafricaines.18387

jealous.

Like the tiny bloodsucking mosquito, when in firefly form, the Adze travels through keyholes, cracks in walls, or under closed doors at night. Once in the home, it would suck blood from people as they slept, making them fall sick and die. In this context, the adze more closely resembles the European concept of the vampire. However, there exists no defense against an Adze. Scholars believe that tales of the creature and its effects were likely an attempt to describe the potentially deadly effects of mosquitoes and malaria.

Asanbosam of West Africa

The legends of the Asanbosam of West Africa reportedly date back as far as the 18th century. The Asanbosam is a legendary creature from West African folklore, believed to live in the forests and rivers of Ghana and Togo.[87] It is described as an entity with iron teeth and sharp claws, which uses these to feed on the blood of its victims. The Asanbosam, similar to the Western version of the vampire, is said to be able to shape-shift into a variety of forms. However, regional differences apply, and the creature may transform into a monkey, a small child, or a spider. Like the common concept of the vampire, the Asanbosam possesses batlike features and is said to have the ability to fly.[88]

According to legend, the Asanbosam preys on humans who venture too far into its territory, particularly those who are alone and vulnerable. It is also said to have a penchant for stealing children. The Asanbosam is believed to have an insatiable appetite for human blood and is said to be particularly fond of children. It is said to lurk in the trees and swoop to snatch unsuspecting victims, often leaving marks on their necks where it has bitten them. When not feeding, they are said to sharpen their fangs upon rocks.[89]

---

87   Konstantinos (1996). Vampires: The Occult Truth. Llewellyn Worldwide. p. 27.
88   [88] Holiday (2010-01-12). "Asanbosam and Sasabonsam". Vampires.

The Asanbosam has been a source of fear in many African cultures for centuries. It is said to be particularly active during the night and can be heard in the forests wailing and cawing. Some believe that the only way to protect oneself from the Asanbosam is to always carry a knife or sharp object with you. In some areas, it is said that the Asanbosam will only attack humans who are not wearing the proper clothing or adornments. Certain colors and symbols are believed to ward off the creature and keep it away. In order to protect themselves from the Asanbosam, some people will wear protective charms or carry talismans with them.

The Asanbosam is a creature that has caused fear in many cultures for centuries. Communities in their territories share stories of the blood sucking tree dwellers. Although it is thought to be a vampire, its exact nature and purpose remain a mystery. Local guides keep a close watch on the treetops for the creatures.

The West African belief in vampires is an ancient belief system rooted in spiritual and cultural traditions. Vampires are believed to be powerful spirits of the dead who return to the living world to cause mischief and harm. Vampires are seen as evil forces that can possess people and animals, bringing misfortune, sickness, death, and destruction to their victims. It is believed that the power of prayer and ritual can defeat vampires and that charms, herbs, and amulets can repel them.

Middle East

The Middle Eastern concept of the vampire is fascinating and has been the subject of many stories and legends throughout the centuries. It is a powerful figure who has fascinated and terrified people for centuries. The Middle Eastern concept of the vampire is quite different from that of other cultures. Unlike the popular image of a pale, undead creature with sharp fangs and an insatiable thirst for human blood, the Middle Eastern

---

89   Eleanor Ferron, Leo Glass, James Jacobs, Jason Keeley, and Owen K.C. Stephens. (2019). "Adventure Toolbox". Cult of Cinders, p. 80.

vampire is far more sinister and mysterious.

In many Middle Eastern legends, the vampire is associated with a supernatural being that can take the form of a human, an animal, or a creature from the spiritual realm. This creature is often said to bring harm to those who cross its path. It is believed that the vampire can control the minds and bodies of its victims, compelling them to do its bidding. Furthermore, it is thought that vampires possess great powers of transformation and can exist in many forms. Such tales have been passed down through generations and continue to haunt our imagination.

Jinn

The Middle Eastern vampire is traditionally known as the Jinn, which is an ancient spirit or supernatural creature in Islamic and pre-Islamic folklore. To Western cultures, the Djinn, or Jinn, is equated with a genie. As such, the genie in the lamp is the common icon associated with the Middle Eastern Jinn. Genie is the anglicized version of Jinn, however, like the spirits of Africa and other early cultures, the Jinn are neither inherently good nor evil. This belief is linked to the blending of other cultural pagan beliefs that have been incorporated into Islamic beliefs.[90]

It is believed that the Jinn is a creature capable of traveling between worlds, shapeshifting, and controlling elements of nature. Folklore relates that the Jinn has been on earth long before the creation of humans. It is further believed that the Jinn is capable of inflicting harm and illness upon humans, and some even claim that the Jinn can take the form of a vampire. The thesaurus reads:

"Djinn noun - (Islam) an invisible spirit mentioned in the Koran and believed by Muslims to inhabit the earth and influence mankind by appearing in the form of humans or animals. Vampires and djinn are semantically related. In some cases, you can use "Vampire" instead of the noun 'Djinn.'"[91]

---

90   McAuliffe, Jane Dammen (2005). *Encyclopaedia of the Qurʾān*. Vol. 3. Brill. p. 45.

According to Middle Eastern folklore, a Jinn vampire is a creature that feeds on human blood and soul and is capable of draining life energy from its victims. This creature is said to be invisible or is usually seen in the form of a large black cloud or a dark figure. One could question the similarity to "shadow figures" in paranormal beliefs. Traditionally, the Jinn is often associated with dark magic and malevolent intentions and is believed to be a force of evil. The Jinn vampire is said to be able to move at incredible speeds and can even fly. It is believed that to protect oneself from the Jinn, one should recite certain prayers and verses from the Quran. It is also said that a person should never look directly at the Jinn, or it may attack them.

The Ghul

The Ghul is another creature of terror, often found in Middle Eastern folklore. It is said to be a shapeshifting creature that can take the form of a hyena, jackal, or antelope. It is believed to inhabit desolate places, such as graveyards and ruins, and is known to have a taste for human flesh. The Ghul is typically depicted as a large, humanoid-like creature with the head of a hyena, an antelope's haunches, and a bat's wings. Its skin is pale, its eyes are red, and it has long, razor-sharp claws. It is said to have an overpowering stench that can be detected from miles away. The concept of the Ghoul is similar to the early vampire ideas of revenants in European cultures.

The word ghoul originates from pre-Islamic culture. The Arabic Ghūl, in popular legend, is a demonic being believed to inhabit burial grounds and other deserted places.[92] In ancient Arabic folklore, Ghūls were believed to be part of a diabolical class of jinn (spirits) and were said to be the offspring of Iblīs, the prince of darkness in Islam. It was believed that they were

---

91 [91]The world's favorite online thesaurus! Thesaurus.com. (n.d.). https://www.thesaurus.com/
92 [92] El-Zein, Amira (2009). Islam, Arabs, and the intelligent world of the jinn. Contemporary Issues in the Middle East (1st ed.). Syracuse, N.Y.: Syracuse University Press. p. 139

capable of constantly changing their form, but their presence was always recognizable by their unalterable sign—ass's hooves. Ancient people believed that Ghūlahs were female and were often confused with the Si'lā, also female; however, the Si'lā was a witchlike species of Jinn, rather than a vampire. She is considered a most malevolent form of Jinn and is considered a Hag. Folklore relates that a Ghūl would stalk the desert, often in the guise of an attractive woman, attempting to distract travelers and, upon success, kill and eat them. The only defense one had against a Ghūl was to strike it dead in one blow; a second blow would only bring it back to life again.

The Ghūl, a prominent figure in the Bedouin imagination, was featured in pre-Islamic Arabic poetry, notably that of *Ta'abbaṭa Sharran*. In North Africa, it was seamlessly incorporated into an ancient Berber folklore which was already replete with demons and other supernatural beings. In modern times, Arabs utilize the term Ghūl to refer to either a human or a demonic cannibal, and it is often employed to deter disobedient children. Anglicized as a Ghoul, the term entered English culture and was further characterized as a creature that scavenges graves and consumes both corpses and children. In the West, ghouls have no specific image and have been described by Edgar Allan Poe as

"They are neither man nor woman—
They are neither brute nor human—
They are Ghouls:"[93]

Legend attests that they assume disguises, ride on dogs and hares, and set fires at night to lure travelers away from the main roads."[94] Like the vampire, the Ghul is most active at night when it is said to prowl the streets in search of its prey. It is further believed to be able to hypnotize its victims and lure

---

93   Bates, C. F. (2010b). Cambridge Book of Poetry and Song: Selected from English and American authors. Nabu Press.
94   Encyclopædia Britannica, inc. (n.d.). Ghoul. Encyclopædia Britannica. https://www.britannica.com/topic/ghoul

them to their doom. Once the Ghul has its victim in its grasp, it is said to devour their flesh, leaving only the bones behind.

The Ghul is an enduring myth that has been passed down through generations in Middle Eastern cultures. It is a powerful reminder of the power of fear and the unknown and serves as a warning to those who are brave enough to venture into the dark unknown.

Chapter 8: Vampires of North America

The European fascination with the vampire in the 19th century extended across the proverbial pond to America. As Polidori's *The Vampyre* presented a romanticized image to surpass the old peasant tales of revenants, so too did the vampire become alluring in America. No longer was the vampire just a peasant's tale of a revenant, but a symbol of romance and glamour. Polidori's The *Vampyre* brought this new image of the vampire to life, captivating readers both in Europe and America alike. It was this romanticized take on the creature that sparked a new fascination with vampires in America. With its dark and mysterious allure, the vampire quickly became an iconic figure in American culture. Even today, vampires continue to be popular figures in literature, film, and television.

The Black Vampire

To most modern people, Blade, portrayed by Wesley Snipes in the film adaptation of the Marvel comic strip of the same name, is the first legitimate vampire of color. The comics were created by Marv Wolfman and first appeared in the 1973 comic book *The Tomb of Dracula*. While only a supporting character, he went on to have his own storylines. In 1998, the film was released, starring Wesley Snipes in the pivotal role.[95] However, Blade was not the first vampire of color to debut in North American literature.

Uriah Derick D'Arcy's *The Black Vampyre: A Legend of St. Domingo*, first published in the early 1800s, is an intriguing parody of Polidori's *The Vampyre*.[96] What makes it so intriguing is the fact that D'Arcy's work challenges societal norms of the time by introducing a vampire of racial origins as the main character. This bold move was not a common occurrence in literature during this era and is a testament to the

---

95 Turan, Kenneth (November 6, 1992). "Blade to Snipes' Heat". The Los Angeles Times. Archived from the original on March 6, 2016.
96 D'Arcy, Uriah (1819). *The Black Vampyre*.

bravery and creativity of D'Arcy as a writer. It is no wonder then that *The Black Vampyre: A Legend of St. Domingo* has since become a classic piece of Gothic literature, still captivating readers today after over two centuries.

Similar to other authors who used the archetype of the vampire as political and societal statements, so too did D'Arcy. Within the context of this story, the vampire is a slave who was murdered by his owner and returned to exact his vengeance upon him. As a common power among vampires is the ability to transform the victim into a follower, the irony is not lost. Not only does this story personify the ravages of slavery but also the revolt against the capitalist mindset driving the institution.[97]

Strongly connected to Haitian spiritual beliefs, this story blends traditional African religion and Catholicism.[98] *The Black Vampyre: A Legend of St. Domingo* contains elements both of biblical and mythological references. For example, it speaks strongly in reference to Obeah practices of Haitian spiritual beliefs. Such practices incorporate a kind of sorcery or magic in ritual. Furthermore, such traditional practices align the concept of the vampire to that of a zombie or undead revenant. As such, zombies represent a "close Cousin" of the vampire and equally represent the early fears of slavery and rebellion against the institution.

New England Vampire Panic

Despite the romanticism of the vampire, American society retained a superstitious fear of such creatures of the night. There is an old adage that states, "Life imitates art." An unbelievable event took hold in New England at the turn of the 19th century, proving that truth is indeed stranger than fiction.

The New England Vampire Panic was a period of hysteria in the late 1800s – early 1900s in parts of New England, caused

---

[97] Faherty, Duncan (2019). "The Black Vampyre; A Legend of St. Domingo (1819)". Just Teach One.
[98] Rey, Terry; Richman, Karen (August 20, 2010). "The Somatics of Syncretism: Tying Body and Soul in Haitian Religion". Studies in Religion/Sciences Religieuses. 39 (3): 379–403.

by tuberculosis, primarily among rural communities.[99] Centered around the belief that people might become vampires after death, these vampires could be responsible for spreading both physical and mental illness. Such a belief is largely based on superstition and folklore. Regardless, it led to a number of strange and sometimes violent practices, including exhuming recently deceased family members, conducting rituals to prevent them from becoming vampires, and burning the bodies of suspected vampires. Retired Civil War Colonel Henry Steel Olcott touted the benefits of cremation and remarked that "there are no vampires save countries where the dead are buried."[100]

The Mercy Brown case occurred in 1892 in Exeter, Rhode Island. It remains the most notorious case in the vampire panic. As such, Rhode Island became the Vampire Capital of the time. The Brown family were farmers when tragedy struck. In 1883, Farmer Brown's wife, Mary, died from a mysterious illness, and a mere six months later, his twenty-year-old daughter, Mary Olive, fell ill with the same illness and perished. Approximately ten years later, Farmer Brown's daughter Mercy and son Edwin fell ill as well.[101] Mercy succumbed to her illness on January 17, 1892. Meanwhile, Edwin, who had once been a strapping lad, languished in his sick bed.

The townsfolk began to whisper. The local doctor informed Farmer Brown that consumption, now called tuberculosis, was the culprit of taking his family. Once upon a time, Tuberculosis was considered "Galloping Consumption" due to the rapidity with which it was transmitted. Tuberculosis is a wasting disease

---

99 Tucker, Abigail. "The Great New England Vampire Panic". Smithsonian magazine. No. October 2012.
100 Horowitz, M. (2013, November 9). How the occult brought cremation to America. HuffPost. https://www.huffpost.com/entry/how-the-occult-brought-cr_b_3880620#:~:text=%22If%20any%20%5Bfurther%20reason%5D,not%20hear%20of%20Hindu%20vampires.%22
101 Robinson, C. T. (2023, April 3). When Rhode Island was "The Vampire Capital of America." New England. https://newengland.com/yankee/history/vampire-mercy-brown-rhode-island/

of the lungs characterized by fever, night sweats, weight loss, and, most notably, a chronic cough and bloody discharge from the lungs. Those afflicted became naturally pale, and the stain of blood on the lips of the patient was reminiscent of vampiric blood drinking. Further, this disease was considered a death warrant.

Despite the official diagnosis, rumors spread that the undead was preying upon poor Farmer Brown's family. The townsfolk were convinced to the point that they trooped to the cemetery and exhumed the bodies of Farmer Brown's wife and two daughters. Edwin was still hanging on to life and the townsfolk believed that one of the deceased women was a vampire sucking the life out of the boy. Only by killing this vampire could his life be saved.

The graves of Mary and Mary Olive, being ten years in the ground revealed only skeletal remains. The grave of Mercy, however, being fresh and cold due to winter's chill revealed something quite different.[102] Such an environment preserved Mercy to the extent that she appeared lifelike. Her liver and heart were removed by the townsfolk and burned. The ashes were mixed into a drink and given to young Edwin as a curative. However, he perished two months later.

Mercy did not remain alone in her vampiric status. As tuberculosis tore through the New England states, tales of vampires also spread. The most common reaction was to burn the organs of the "vampire" as a preventative against others being attacked. Such measures were common folk medicine. In New England, belief in vampires was widespread, and, for some families, lasted well into the twentieth century.

Jewett City Vampires

Children playing near a gravel mine in the early 1990s in Jewett City, Connecticut, returned home with a skull. Initially believed to be the victim of then serial killer, Michael Ross, and

---

102 Editor Account. (n.d.). Have Mercy... The Rhode Island Historical Society. https://www.rihs.org/have-mercy/

immediately began an investigation of the area. However, the remains came from a lost family graveyard belonging to the Ray and Walton family.

As with the tale of Mercy Brown, a member of the Ray family contracted tuberculosis in the mid-19th century. The first fatality of the family was Lemuel Ray, a 24-year-old son. His father, Henry passed away seven years later and was quickly followed by two other Ray sons.[103] The particular grave uncovered in the 1990s was that of JB. This coffin contained evidence of body disruption. While medical evidence upholds the theory that the occupant died from tuberculosis, this grave was the only one which bore any signs of tampering. Originally buried in the 1790s, this grave was dug up and the head decapitated from its spine. Further, the femurs were placed below the skull to form the skull and crossbones pattern.[104] Such methods were employed to for the same purpose as removing organs and burning them; to stop a vampire in its tracks.

Vampire of Lafayette, Colorado

The Vampire of Lafayette, Colorado dates back to the early twentieth century. Todor Glava immigrated from Romania and settled in Colorado in the early 1900s. Working as a coal miner left him pale and thin. During the peak of the Spanish Influenza epidemic of 1918, Glava passed away in December of that year.

After his death, however, rumors began to circulate that Glava was more sinister than previously imagined. Local folklore relates that the townsfolk exhumed the body and found that Glava's teeth were abnormally long, and his fingernails had never stopped growing. Coming to the natural conclusion that he must be rising from his grave to feast on the blood of the good townsfolk, they took matters into their own hands and drove a stake through his heart.[105]

---

103 [103]Bendici, Ray. "Jewett City Vampires, Griswold". www.damnedct.com. Damned Connecticut.
104 [104] Ibid
105 [105] Kelseynistel. (2021, September 16). Legend says a vampire is buried in this Colorado cemetery. Townsquare Fort Collins.

While there is no historical evidence to support this story, the legend remains. Further, growing by his grave is one lone spindly tree. Rumor relates that the tree sprouted from the stake driven through Glava's heart. According to author Mark Collins Jenkins in his book Vampire Forensics, is the close correlation between disease and vampires.[106] To those unacquainted with how diseases spread it may have been easier to put the blame upon vampires.

Jacques St. Germaine- The Vampire of New Orleans

Who was Jacques St. Germain? An eccentric aristocrat, a charlatan, or maybe a vampire? There is truly little historical information about the New Orleans legend. Conversely, an abundance of information exists regarding the Comte St. Germain of 1700s France. Notable men such as Voltaire and King Louis XV claim to have known his acquaintance. Voltaire went so far as to claim that "He is a man who knows everything and who never dies." Historic records indicate that he was born in 1710 and died in 1784.[107] Yet, people claim to have seen the Comte as late as 1970. As was ever so fashionable in the 1700s, the Comte was an alchemist, and rumors claim he grew diamonds. To add to his character, legend states that he spoke six languages, was a violin virtuoso, and was a skilled artist. As wonderful as he may appear, records claim he died in 1784, so how did he come to live in New Orleans 200 years later?

Oral tradition marks Jacques as a French immigrant who came to New Orleans around the turn of the twentieth century (although a precise date has yet to be discovered). He moved into a home off Royal Street and soon insinuated himself into his community. Jacques claimed to have been descended from the beloved Comte St. Germain. Like his supposed namesake,

---

https://townsquarenoco.com/legend-says-a-vampire-is-buried-in-this-colorado-cemetery/
106   Jenkins, M. (2011). Vampire Forensics: Uncovering the origins of an enduring legend. National Geographic.
107   Oakley, I. C. (1927). The Comte de St. Germain: The Secret of Kings.

he also was quite a charmer. He threw grand parties and invited only the most prestigious of guests.[108] His knowledge of history was quite extensive to the point of speaking as a witness to the greatest events in the world. Although his fetes were well catered with the best of food, Jacques never ate. Although plenty of his guests noticed this peculiarity, no one seemed to care. That is until events took a dark turn.

Vampire enthusiasts throughout New Orleans relate a sordid tale. During one of his popular parties, Jacques asked a lovely woman to join him on the balcony. While there, the legend relates that he tried to bite her neck. The shocked woman, in an attempt to escape, jumped over the balcony railing to the pavement below. She survived the fall and was found with blood trickling down her neck. She was in a state of terror and was quickly surrounded by passers-by, and the police were fetched. The poor woman was taken to the hospital and, all the while, held to her story that she had been bitten by her mysterious host. Of course, the police would not bather such an affluent man at such a late hour and asked him to come to the station in the morning to answer a few questions. He never arrived. That night, Jacques St. Germain disappeared.

Most of Jacques' belongings were left behind in his home. When the police arrived to search the dwelling, they were shocked at what they found. The second floor contained open yet corked wine bottles filled with a mixture of wine and, as rumor states, large amounts of human blood. Further, police discovered many articles of clothing from different time periods, all stained with blood. No food was to be found within his home, nor any utensils. Also missing was Jacques St. Germain. He never returned to his home.

According to a New Orleans city directory, a man by the name of Jacques St. Germain lived in the city in 1895. Further, Jean Jacques St. Germain died at the age of 27 in 1823 in New

---

108 [108]Murphy, Michael (2015-10-01). "Chapter 3: Vampires". Fear Dat New Orleans: A Guide to the Voodoo, Vampires, Graveyards & Ghosts of the Crescent City. The Countryman Press. pp. 132–135.

Orleans. Could they have been the same man? Yet another document details the immigration of Jacques Germain, age 52, in 1890 to New Orleans. Further, his occupation is listed as an engineer. Sadly, after a thorough perusal of available online Louisiana historical newspapers, there is no mention of Jacques St. Germain or the horrifying incident of the vampire's kiss. Additionally, upon researching the chain of title for the supposed home for Mr. St. Germain, the results revealed that no such person ever owned the home. With no historical data to correlate with the legends, the story of the New Orleans vampire must, for the present moment, be relegated to the category of legend. But like all legends, there lies a seed of truth. For this legend, the Comte St. Germain of France is the driving force of this story and the storytellers who keep the memory alive.[109]

The Carter Brothers

In 1932, a young female was observed to be in a state of panic as she traversed Royal Street, her progress only briefly interrupted by the intervention of a police officer. Upon questioning, she relayed a seemingly implausible tale of being bound by two brothers, alongside several other captives, and held captive for the purpose of consuming their blood. Despite the incredulity of the police, they agreed to accompany her to the residence located at the corner of Royal and St. Ann. Upon arriving at the Carter brothers' home, the police were appalled to discover, as the female had described, four other victims in a state of near-death, tied to chairs in one of the rooms.[110]

It was observed that all victims had their wrists bound with bandages, which were moist and stained with blood. Furthermore, two more bodies, wrapped in blankets, were located in another room. The apartment was permeated with the

---

109 [109] Link to the historic property with the chain of ownership: https://www.hnoc.org/vcs/property_info.php?lot=22915
110 Team, Y. A. E. (2020, May 19). The forgotten history of two new Orleans vampires. Yesterday's America. https://yesterdaysamerica.com/the-forgotten-history-of-two-new-orleans-vampires/

unmistakable and suffocating odor of death. It was noted that the brothers would leave the premises early each morning, just before daybreak, and return every evening just after dark. Upon their return, they would remove the bandages from each of the captives' wrists and, using a knife, reopen the wounds until blood flowed freely from the cuts. They would then catch the blood in cups from which they would drink until their hunger was sated. Following this, the brothers would redress the wounds with fresh bandages. It was observed that they spoke very little and showed no concern for the well-being of their victims, treating them as nothing more than a food source destined for certain death.

Unbeknownst to John and Wayne Carter, the girl had escaped. Consequently, when the two brothers returned to their usual routine, the police were waiting for them. Upon their apprehension, the brothers confessed almost immediately, imploring to be put to death. They informed the authorities that they were, in fact, vampires and that, if released, they would have no other choice but to continue to take lives due to their insatiable thirst for blood. It is reported that the brothers were tried as serial killers, found guilty, and eventually executed.[111]

The Vampire of Sacramento

Richard Trenton Chase, known as "The Vampire Killer of Sacramento", was responsible for the deaths of six known victims. Born on May 23rd, 1950, in Sacramento, California, Chase exhibited troubling behavior from a young age, such as setting fires, wetting the bed, and torturing animals. As he grew older, he began to abuse drugs and alcohol, which led to him developing hypochondria.[112]

This caused him to tell doctors that his pulmonary artery had been stolen, his heart would stop beating, and that his blood

---

111 [111]History of vampires in New Orleans. Where Y'at New Orleans. (n.d.). https://www.whereyat.com/a-vampire-culture-thats-to-die-for
112 [112] Bovsun, Mara (January 2, 2010). "Just crazy for blood: Richard Trenton Chase, a.k.a. the Vampire of Sacramento". New York Daily News.

was turning to powder.[113] He had no social life or girlfriends and instead spent his time capturing and killing animals, which he then ate raw or blended up. In 1976, he was hospitalized for blood poisoning after injecting himself with the blood from a rabbit he had killed.

Many patients and nurses were frightened by him and referred to him as Dracula due to his frequent appearance with blood smeared on his face. It was later discovered that he had been biting the heads of birds and sucking their blood. After taking medication, he was released, but a year later, he was found in a field near Lake Tahoe, Nevada, naked and covered in cow's blood. The incident was reported, but no further action was taken.[114]

Native American

The Native Americans have many different vampire-like creatures of legend spread across various tribes. Some tribes, such as the Hopi and the Ojibwe, believe that there are malevolent spirits that could take the form of animals in order to attack people. The Navajo believe that there are the undead spirits of evil people, and the Apache believe that vampires are created when a dead person has their skin removed and their body filled with evil spirits. Other Native American tribes have their own vampire-like legends.

For example, the Pomo believe that such beings are created when a person dies with unfinished business, and the Sioux believe that they are created when a person dies with a powerful spiritual presence—one so powerful that it can return from the dead. In some tribes, such as the Lenape, it is believed that vampires are created when a person dies without a proper burial. The Cree believe that vampires are created when a person's body is left exposed to the elements. Finally, the Zuni

113   [113] Amanda Howard, Martin Smith: River of Blood, Universal Publishers (August 30, 2004), ISBN 978-1-58112-518-4, pp. 82
114   [114] Richard Trenton Chase. Crime Museum. (2021, August 13). https://www.crimemuseum.org/crime-library/serial-killers/richard-trenton-chase/

believe that such beings are created when a person dies with a debt of blood owed to them. The souls of the dead will then return to take revenge on the living.

It has been observed that there are numerous humanoid monsters in Native American folklore that were believed to hunt and prey on humans, including some that rise from the dead. While these creatures might be considered to be 'vampires' in a broader sense, as they do not possess the distinctive characteristics of European vampires, such as an association with bats, an inability to withstand sunlight, being killed by a stake through the heart, casting no shadow or reflection, and weaknesses to garlic and running water. Moreover, the most defining feature of a vampire is the ability to turn a victim into another vampire by biting him or her; this is not present in traditional Native American folklore.[115]

Windigo

The Windigos are a legendary species of cannibalistic ice giants that are present in the folklore of various Northern Algonquian Indian tribes who were located along the East Coast of America and Canada.[116] Additionally, they are referred to as Chenoo in the Micmac language, Giwakwa in the Abenaki language, and other names in other tribes. According to most versions of the legend, Windigos were once humans who had committed an atrocity such as cannibalism, leading to their hearts turning to ice. In other legends, it is stated that evil wizards had the power to transform people into Windigos. Regardless, the monsters were said to roam the wilderness, consuming any human they encountered until their demise.

Like the common vampire myth, Wendigo's were also once

---

115   [115] Native American vampires of myth and legend. Native American Vampire Characters of Myth and Legend (American Indian Vampires and Vampire-Like Monsters). (n.d.). http://www.native-languages.org/native-vampires.htm
116   [116] Zarka, Emily (October 17, 2019). "Windigo: The Flesh-Eating Monster of Native American Legend". Monstrum. Season 1. Episode 13. PBS Digital Studios

human. Further, similar to the earlier mythos, vampires were also a result of sin, and they, too, are cursed to wander the land preying on human blood. According to legend, the Windigo is a human that is coated in ice (cold like a vampire) and resides within the monster. The human body is located where the heart of the monster would be and, like the vampire, must be killed to defeat the monster, similar to a stake through the heart.

However, a few legends do have happier endings where the Windigo is able to be transformed back into a human. Some myths claim that the human is able to be rescued from the heart of the Windigo. Unfortunately, it is more likely that once a person is possessed by the spirit of a Windigo, their only true escape is death.

Skinwalker

It is said that Skinwalkers, fearsome shapeshifting monsters of Navajo legend, are created when humans partake in forbidden evil magic and/or commit heinous crimes, such as the murder of one's own parents. These creatures are more akin to European legends of werewolves than vampires, as they are primarily known for assuming the form of animals at night to prey upon humans before reverting back to their human form during the day. However, they also possess certain traits that are reminiscent of vampires, such as an aversion to sunlight, immunity to regular weapons, the ability to read minds, and the power to hypnotize and exert control over those who look them in the eyes.

Indigenous Navajo people are reluctant to discuss the Skinwalker as there is a belief that to even discussing the creature will cause it to appear. Due to their deep-held spiritual beliefs on the subject, the Skinwalker legend is not well understood by outsiders.[117] However, there are some similarities between this shadowy myth and that of the vampire.

---

117   Hampton, Carol M. "Book Review: Some Kind of Power: Navajo Children's Skinwalker Narratives" in Western Historical Quarterly. 1 July 1986.

Like early accounts of vampires transforming into dogs, one of the most common forms of animal attributed to the Skinwalker is the wolf or coyote. Further, both tend to be nocturnal and possess extraordinary strength and speed.

Contrary to vampire lore, the most effective way to defeat a Skinwalker is to discover its true identity. Yet, similar to vampire legends, this renders it vulnerable during the day, like a vampire in its coffin. In some stories, medicine men are able to create sacred weapons that can be used to vanquish a Skinwalker. The Skinwalker legend is not one to be taken lightly, as stories still abound today of attacks from this beast.

Mosquito Man

Many tribes have legends concerning man-eating monsters that were transformed into mosquitoes, thus continuing to feed on people, albeit in a less lethal manner. The Northwest Coast tribes have some particularly gruesome versions of this legend, in which the original monster, Mosquito Man, inserts his proboscis into a person's head and extracts their brains, often so discreetly that those around him do not even realize their companion is deceased. An example of such a legend, as told by the Haida, is of a baby being passed around at a gathering, where Mosquito Man clandestinely sucks its brains out before passing it on to the next person, who is aghast to discover that the infant is both brainless and deceased.

It is not uncommon that mosquitoes were seen as enemies of humankind by the early Indigenous tribes. As such, many legends feature blood-sucking or man-eating legends based upon this little pest. Interestingly, despite the Mosquito Man legend of the Pacific Northwest, local tribal clans such as the Haida and Gitxsan, both of Canada, adopted the mosquito as their crest. Meanwhile the Creek tribe of the East Coast performs a mosquito dance in which dancers are pricked with pins. Such traditions reflect the role blood played in early cultures as a life force. While the Mosquito Man sucks out the brains of his victims, his actions of preying on humans harkens back to that of the vampire.

Two-Face

It has been reported that the Sioux and other Plains tribes have entities in their mythology that bear resemblance to humans yet possess a second face on the back of their heads. Making eye contact with these creatures is said to either result in instant death or paralysis, leaving the individual vulnerable to being stabbed to death with their sharp elbows. As such, the only way to avoid such a fate is to ensure that one never meets their gaze.

Depending on the tradition, there may be only one Two-Face (which may be either female or male) or a whole race of them. The misdeeds attributed to the Two-Face range from murder and mutilation to cannibalism, kidnapping, and even frightening children. While vampires do not traditionally have a face on the back of their heads, legends do relate that they have the ability to transfix their victims and hold mental control over them. Further, a parallel may be drawn between the vampire and Two-Face in that traditionally, the vampire presents itself as a normal human, often wealthy and charming, yet its other face is that of a cold-blooded killer.

Skadegamutc

The Wabanaki tribes of New England are said to be home to Skadegamutc (skuh-deh-guh-mooch), or ghost witches. These creatures are believed to be created when an evil sorcerer dies, at which point they refuse to remain dead and begin to rise from the grave like the early revenants at night to prey on humans. During the day, like the vampire, a ghost witch appears to be an ordinary corpse and can only be destroyed permanently by fire.[118]

By night, the corpse reanimates and embarks upon a quest for human prey. To facilitate this, the Ghost-Witch assumes the form of a ball of light instead of a bat, allowing it to traverse vast distances in a short period of time. Furthermore, it is

---

118   [118] Native American Legends: SKADEGAMUTC (ghost-witch). Skadegamutc, the Ghost-witch. (n.d.). http://www.native-languages.org/skadegamutc.htm

endowed with immense strength. Upon locating a target, the monster launches an attack from a higher altitude. Subsequently, it slaughters its victim, consuming their warm flesh and blood.

It is widely believed that, much like the Vampire of Eastern and Central Europe, the Skadegamutc is vulnerable during the day. However, according to Wabanaki folklore, the Skadegamutc cannot be harmed by weapons. While some legends suggest that arrows may ward off or even frighten the creature away, the efficacy of this method is not known. The only sure way to destroy the Ghost-Witch is to burn the creature to charred ashes and scatter the ashes to the four winds, thus preventing the revenant from returning and exacting its revenge upon those who sought to destroy it.

American vampire lore has a unique identity all its own, characterized by the cultural amalgamation of ideas and influences. This includes elements such as the Native American Wendigo, a monster-like creature that feeds on human flesh, and the Haitian Voodoo practices of using blood sacrifice to ward off evil spirits. Moreover, tales of vampires reflect the anxieties of immigrants coming to America and their fears of being persecuted and misunderstood in their new home. Throughout history, American vampire lore has served as a form of storytelling that reflects our collective hopes and fears.

Chapter 9 Vampires of South America

Vampire folklore is not as prevalent in South America as it is in Western Europe or North America, yet some general beliefs of vampirism have been present in this part of the world for centuries. One of the most striking examples of this is the belief that vampire bats originated in the Southern and Central Americas. It is no wonder that people from every corner of the world find themselves drawn to these mysterious creatures and the stories that follow them. Whether it is the idea of immortality, supernatural powers, or something else entirely, there always seems to be something about vampires that sparks our fascination and draws us in.[119]

Vampires have been featured in many diverse cultures around the world throughout history, though the exact nature of their powers and abilities varies greatly. In some stories, vampires are portrayed as powerful, immortal creatures that can fly and control the minds of mortals. In other tales, their abilities are more subtle, and they might be able to manipulate emotions or influence dreams. Nevertheless, it is clear that vampires have been a source of fascination for many years. They represent a fascinating mix of both fear and desire, which is why they remain such a compelling topic even today.

El Chupacabra

The Chupacabra is a legendary creature believed to inhabit parts of the Americas, with the first sightings reported in Puerto Rico. It is described as a heavy creature, the size of a small bear, with a row of spines reaching from the neck to the base of the tail. It has leathery or scaly greenish-gray skin and is said to have a dog or panther-like face with a forked tongue. It is said to have large, glowing red eyes and to leave behind a sulfuric stench.

The name derives from the Spanish word *Chupar,* meaning to

---

119   Miranda L. Vampires in South America. Great Gothic Giggle. https://greatgothicgiggle.home.blog/2019/03/28/vampires-in-south-america/.

suck, and *Cabra,* meaning goat. In theory, it can be loosely translated to goatsucker. Reports of attacks on animals, especially goats, have been made, with the creatures draining the animals of their blood. Ironically, the Chupacabra is traditionally more likened to the North American legend of Sasquatch rather than the vampire despite its predilection for draining the blood of its victims. However, this association is now changing, with the creatures becoming viewed as more vampirical in nature.

The first official report of the beast occurred in 1975 in Moca, Puerto Rico. These killings were first blamed on the Vampire of Moca.[120] However, later attacks upon livestock in March 1995 were blamed on the Chupacabra. Eight sheep had been found deceased and untouched except for two puncture wounds on their chests and a curious lack of blood. In August of that year, an eyewitness from a village in which as many as 150 farm animals and pets had been killed came forward to describe the creature. According to first reports, witnesses described the creature as a large reptilian with red eyes. Researcher Benjamin Radford, in his book *Tracking the Chupacabra,* states that this description we based on the character "Sil" from the 1995 horror film, *Species.*[121]

However, no living specimens were found in any of these cases. Soon reports of other curious animal deaths began flooding in areas in South America. Reports also began to spring up as far north as America, where witnesses reported them as standing on four legs with features closely resembling a canine. As recently as 2018, reports of suspected Chupacabras came out of Manipur, India; however, feral street dogs were blamed for these deaths.[122] Today, the Chupacabra remains a creature shrouded in mystery, and its existence has yet to be

---

120   [120] Wagner, Stephen (2000). "Encounters with Chupacabras". About.com
121   Radford, Benjamin (2011). Tracking the Chupacabra: The Vampire Beast in Fact, Fiction and Folklore
122   Karmakar, Rahul (8 December 2018). "On the mystery of livestock deaths in Manipur" (Online news article). The Hindu.

proven.

El Coco

Also known as the "bogeyman," El Coco is said to be a creature that hides beneath beds and in closets, waiting to snatch away naughty children and take them to the underworld. The attributes of El Coco vary somewhat from the more traditional vampire legend and are predominately thought to be a story to keep children from misbehaving.

Parents invoke El Coco in areas of Latin America as a way to discourage their children from misbehaving. Children are told that if they disobey their parents, El Coco will come to snatch them away and eat them. The thought of being eaten by a monster is typically enough to scare a child into behaving. Such concepts are quite common in many cultures throughout the world.

Around the globe, societies have used the archetype of a demon, god, or monster to teach children the importance of being well-behaved. The moral of the story is that by giving in to base emotions such as anger, one is taken over by a larger monster, and all vestiges of the child will soon disappear.

One of the oldest children's rhyme about El Coco states:
Duérmete niño, duérmete ya...
Que viene el Coco y te comerá
Sleep child, sleep or else...
Coco will come and eat you.

This rhyme was written by Juan Caxés in the 17th century work *Auto de los desposorios de la Virgen*[123]. It is the concept that El Coco will eat children that have equated it with the legend of the vampire. While there is not a general consensus on the appearance of El Coco, its ability to shapeshift is another shared feature of the vampire.

---

[123] Caxesi, Juan. Desposorios (Los) de la Virgen. Auto sacramental. Biblioteca Nacional de España, Madrid
https://manos.net/manuscripts/bne/15-216-desposorios-los-de-la-virgen-auto-sacramental?locale=es

El Duende

"Do not go to the bush to cut firewood nor look for coconut husks, or El Dueno del Monte" will get you." This was a common threat in the 1940s and 50s, which mom would use when she needed the children at home for some chores rather than going to the bush. This creature is said to be a small, mischievous goblin-like creature that loves to play pranks and cause mischief. Those who saw him said he was about 3 feet tall and wore a wide-brimmed hat. Sometimes he wore a red hat and animal skins for clothing.[124]

El Duende is referred to as an evil being. Duendes are mythical characters featured in written and oral traditions in Latin America, Spain, and Europe. In the South American country of Ecuador, there is a popular characterization of this myth that has come to be known as El Duende.[125] This character is identified mainly as a male character that can be a beautiful singing creature, a lucky charm, or an elusive small man who causes mischief and even violence. It is said that the Duende only appears to single women, either on remote roads to rural villages, underneath the nance trees (a shrub native of Costa Rica, El Salvador, Honduras, Mexico, and Nicaragua related to the plant family Malpigiaceas, and which produces a delicious yellow fruit about the size of the fruit of a coffee bean), or when women are alone in their houses.

The meanings of the stories about this figure are described differently depending on the region and the person telling the story. However, a salient and recurring characterization of El Duende in Ecuador describes him as particularly dangerous for women. The duende is reported as being an enamorado, or a playboy, who offers many gifts and wealth to the girls so that

---

[124] NUÑEZ, A. (n.d.). "El Duende"- San Pedro Folklore. "El duende"- san pedro folklore, 25 years ago, history of San Pedro, Ambergris Caye, Belize. https://ambergriscaye.com/25years/elduende.html
[125] Penafiel, C. (n.d.). El Duende. University of New Mexico. https://digitalrepository.unm.edu/cgi/viewcontent.cgi?article=1055&context=ltam_etds

they go away with him. If a girl does not recognize the duende and accepts anything he offers her, then she will remain enchanted by the evil powers of the Duende. This aspect of the creature echoes the mesmeric enchantment of the vampire. Legend says that the vampire has the ability to hypnotize victims into doing his bidding.

El Cadejo

Interestingly, El Cadejo legends differ from the traditional vampire mythos seen in other parts of the world. However, it does share a similar lore in that it can take the form of a dog. Further, legend states that this creature possesses magical powers. El Cadejo can appear as either white or black depending upon its nature of good or evil.[126]

El Cadejo is a legendary creature from Central American folklore. It is said to be a large dog with glowing red eyes that appears at night to protect travelers from danger. The white Cadejo is said to be a guardian of the dead and a protector of children. However, the back, or evil, Cadejo, it is said, aims to kill unwitting travelers who happen upon it. It is further believed that. Like vampires of previous eras, the black Cadejo eats babies.

Like the vampire, El Cadejo appears at night. The creature is described as being incredibly strong and fast, and it is said to be able to appear and disappear at will. It is believed that El Cadejo can bring either good or bad luck, depending on how it is treated. It is also said to be able to grant wishes if it is treated with respect.

El Cadejo has been the subject of many stories and legends throughout Central American culture. It is said that if you are fortunate enough to come across El Cadejo with white fur during your travels, you should show it respect and kindness, as it may be able to grant you a wish. Some people even believe that El Cadejo has magical powers, such as the ability to make

---

126   Games and Popular Superstitions of Nicaragua, E.A.P de Guerrero, p. 38, in The Journal of American Folklore, Volume 4, Parts 1-2, 1891

objects move or disappear.

The duality displayed by the varying myth of good and evil of this creature reflects both the attraction and repulsion characteristic of modern vampires. Additionally, like many modern vampire myths, the evil El Cadejo lurks in dark alleys and graveyards, looking for its next victim.

El Arbol Del Vampiro (The Vampire's Tree)

Legend has it that El Panteón de Belen cemetery in Guadalajara, Jalisco, Mexico is home to the infamous vampire's tree! This legend dates back to the 18th century when Mexico was still under Spain's rule. A man named Jorge moved to the area and bought a hacienda, but the townsfolk noticed their animals were dying with their blood drained. One night, they investigated and discovered Jorge biting an animal's neck. They tried to chase him, but he was too fast and escaped. To prevent him from returning, the townsfolk drove a stake through his heart and buried him in El Panteón de Belen.[127]

Surprisingly, a tree began to grow over his tomb. The locals believed that when the tree grew too much and tore, Jorge would return for his revenge. Another version of the legend states that a bruja told the townspeople to use a stake made from an Arbol camichin to stab Jorge in the heart. After burying him, they placed a giant rock over his tomb, which caused a break, and the camichin branch began to grow through the cracks.

Today, the tree stands at least fifteen meters tall, and visitors can take a tour of the cemetery to see it for themselves. Tours are usually in Spanish, but there are English tours at certain times. If you want to take pictures, you will need to pay an extra fee of 250 pesos. Despite a few angry Americans who missed the English tours and did not want to pay the fee, the cemetery has great reviews![128]

---

127 [127]City, M. (2020, June 8). La Escalofriante Historia del árbol del vampiro de guadalajara. MXCity. https://mxcity.mx/2020/06/arbol-del-vampiro-leyenda-guadalajara/

Pishtaco Vampires in Peru

The Pishtaco, a vampire from Peruvian folklore, stands out from other classic vampire tales. Rather than drinking blood, they drain their victims' fat. According to legend, the Pishtaco is a man-like monster from the Andes who preys on Indigenous people for their fat. This fat is then used for a variety of purposes, including soap and candles. The name Pishtaco comes from the Quechua word "pishtay," meaning "to behead, slit throat, or cut into pieces."[129] In pre-Columbian Peruvian culture, fat was viewed as a sign of health, beauty, wealth, and strength, Meanwhile, illnesses were thought to be caused by the loss of body fat.[130]

The legend of the Pishtaco became particularly rooted in folklore when Spanish missionaries settled in Peru during the 1700s. The Conquistadors were accused of killing Indigenous people in order to obtain their fat, and ill practices such as treating wounds with the fat of enemies were seen as abhorrent. The earliest known reference to the Pishtaco Legend is from 1574, when Indigenous people of the area avoided the Spaniards in fear of being killed for their fat.

The legend of the Pishtaco is intertwined with another folktale, known as the Cauchus or Runapmicuc, which translates to "Person who consumes." According to legend, this creature would sneak into people's houses and put them to sleep using a powder made of human bones, then drink their blood from the wound. It is believed that the Pishtaco and Cauchus legends have become one, resulting in a fat-draining vampire.

In 2009, a hoax of Peruvian Gangsters who would kill people to obtain their fat caused an uproar. This gang was ironically given the name "Pishtacos," but it is the Spanish Conquistadors

---

128 [128]Vampires in Latin America. Espooky Tales. (n.d.). https://www.espookytales.com/blog/vampires-in-latin-america/
129 Benson, Elizabeth P.; Cook, Anita Gwynn (2001). Ritual sacrifice in ancient Peru. University of Texas Press.
130 Weismantel, Mary J. (2001). Cholas and pishtacos: stories of race and sex in the Andes. University of Chicago Press.

and missionaries who were truly the bloodthirsty fat stealers, acting upon the Native people with horrifying brutality. It is clear that the original Pishtaco legend was rooted in fact, as human fat was used for a variety of purposes during the Spanish conquest of Peru.[131]

Azéman Vampire

Among some of the most popular vampires in South America is the Azéman of Surinam. Surinam is a country located in the North of Brazil. Interestingly, the Azéman is the name used for both the vampire and werewolf in this region. The creature is able to hide its identity during the day under the disguise of a normal peasant. Villagers believed it entered houses throughout the night by flying through the air. It had the fearsome ability to transform back into its real self during the darkness of the night: a vampire. In this state, it then went on to suck as much blood as it craved from its numerous victims, leading to unresolved cases of murder in the mortal community by the break of daylight.

During the day, Azéman led the community life of an old man and an old woman.[132] Additionally, it has the fascinating and peculiar capability to take off its skin and become a blue ball of light after it transforms into a vampire. The people who were under suspicion of being Azéman were put under high surveyance. Their identity was determined by the excruciating technique of ripping their skin off. The skin was thus shrunk with salt and pepper so that the vampire could not wear its skin on again.

Also, one of the best protection against the Azéman was the use of garlic. Garlic was drunk as it was steamed in hot water beforehand. This way, the herbs turned the victims' blood bitter, making it repulsive to the vampire's taste. sprinkling

---

131   Andrew Whalen (AP) (2009-11-19). "Gang Killed People For Their Fat: Peruvian Police". Huffington Post.
132   Melville J. Herskovits and Frances S. Herskovits (1936) Suriname folk-lore [1], New York: Columbia University Press, page 43

seeds on the ground will cause it to stop whatever it is doing to count them, as it is inexplicably compelled to do so. To stop it from entering one's home, a person can prop a broom across the doorway, as it will create a mystical barrier that the azéman cannot cross.[133]

The Lobishomen

The Lobishomen arise from the Portuguese mythology in Brazil. In Brazil, people usually view it as a werewolf, but in some versions is a ball of fire or a curiously large pig.[134] It has also been said that a Lobishomen has the physical appearance of a small, stumpy, and hunchbacked monkey being. While in human form, however, the creature looks like a normal person, yet, like the classic Nosferatu, it has pointed ears and pale skin.

Like werewolf legends, Lobishomen are believed to shape shift during the full moon. However, it always transforms during the night, like the vampire, and attacks travelers and animals on the road. There are several ways in which a person may become this creature. Similar to traditional vampire and werewolf legends, a bite from the creature or contact with its blood will turn a human into a monster.

Legends state that it took on the regular activity of attacking females, making them nymphomaniacs. It could get easily drunk on blood, making it easy to capture and execute. The first Lobishomen were created through witchcraft or non-proper cohabitation between their parents, such as incest. Despite attempts to eradicate this entity, a small number of Lobishomen have nevertheless escaped to survival.

South American vampires are depicted as mysterious and exotic creatures with their own unique set of powers and abilities. They are often associated with the dark and

---

[133] American Folklore Society, Journal of American Folklore, vol. 30, 242
[134] Harris, Mark (2013). "The Werewolf in between Indians and Whites: Imaginative Frontiers and Mobile Identities in Eighteenth Century Amazonia". Tipití: Journal of the Society for the Anthropology of Lowland South America. 11.

mysterious aspects of the region's culture and history. Portrayed as powerful and dangerous but also as mysterious. They represent the region's exotic and mysterious nature, and their stories are typically used as a source of fear and fascination.

Chapter 10: Vampires in Pop Culture

The influence of vampire lore on popular culture is undeniable. Vampires have been a source of fascination for centuries, and their allure has only grown with time. From Bram Stoker's *Dracula* to Anne Rice's *Interview With the Vampire*, vampires have been a staple of literature and film for generations. The most iconic vampire of all is undoubtedly Count Dracula. He has inspired countless books and movies, including the classic 1931 Universal Pictures film starring Bela Lugosi. Dracula's popularity has endured over the decades, and he has been portrayed in countless ways. He has been portrayed by modern actors Gary Oldman, Christopher Lee, and even Leslie Nielsen in the comedy classic *Dracula: Dead and Loving It*.

Vampires also represent a popular subject on television, particularly in recent years. The CW's long-running series The *Vampire Diaries*, as well as its spinoff *The Originals*, have both been incredibly popular. The HBO series *True Blood* was a major hit and ran for seven seasons, while the Netflix adaptation of Bram Stoker's *Dracula* has been highly acclaimed. Additionally, vampire lore has made its way into the world of video games. The popular *Castlevania* series debuted in the late 1980s and remains a favorite of gamers today. Further, the immensely popular role-playing game *Vampire: The Masquerade* has spawned several sequels and become a cult classic.

Vampires have become a part of pop culture in other ways as well. There are vampire-themed board games, such as *Vampire: The Eternal Struggle*, as well as the previously mentioned vampire-themed card game, *Vampire: The Masquerade*. There are even vampire-themed fashion lines, ranging from clothing to accessories. Vampires have made their way into our lives in many forms, and their influence on popular culture is undeniable. From literature to film, television, video games, and fashion, vampires have become integral to our lives. It is amazing to see how the lore of vampires has managed to remain popular and relevant over the years, and it shows no signs of slowing down anytime soon.

The Vampire in Movies

The vampire became a favorite movie monster in the earliest days of cinema. From the silent film era to the modern age, the vampire continues to captivate audiences with its alluring charm and wicked bite. The first vampire film was the 1922 silent movie *Nosferatu*, directed by F. W. Murnau. The movie follows the plight of a young man who is targeted by a vampire named Count Orlok. The film is considered a classic and a masterpiece of horror. Although it is an unofficial adaptation of Bram Stoker's *Dracula*, it has earned a place as a masterpiece of horror.[135]

Count Orlok, also known as Nosferatu, is a grotesque, wizened figure with a bald head, dark, sunken eyes, and long, sharp fingernails.[136] He travels by night and is often accompanied by rats and bats. Count Orlok is a vampire of immense power, able to control the minds of others and shapeshift into a giant bat or wolf. He possesses the ability to transform into a fog and move through walls, chimneys, and other openings. Although he is a creature of the night, Count Orlok is vulnerable to the light of day. He must avoid the sun at all costs, as it can burn him to ash. In fact, this film was the first to portray a vampire dying from sun exposure.[137]

He is a classic example of the horror genre, and his evil and terrifying presence continues to haunt the night. Former film critic Roger Ebert summed up the film's legacy when he said,

"Here is the story of Dracula before it was buried alive in

---

135 "What's the Big Deal?: Nosferatu (1922) (archived October 13, 2011)". Archived from the original

136 [136] Giesen, Rolf (2019). The Nosferatu Story: The Seminal Horror Film, Its Predecessors, and Its Enduring Legacy. McFarland & Company. ISBN 978-1476672984.

137 [137] Scivally, Bruce (1 September 2015). Dracula FAQ: All That's Left to Know About the Count from Transylvania. Hal Leonard Corporation.

clichés, jokes, TV skits, cartoons and more than thirty other films. *The film is in awe of its material. It seems to really believe in vampires. ...Is Murnau's Nosferatu scary in the modern sense? Not for me. I admire it more for its artistry and ideas, its atmosphere, and images than for its ability to manipulate my emotions like a skillful modern horror film.*"[138]

Eventually, silent movies gave way to what the industry termed "talkies." Talkies are what we watch today, movies in which the audience hears the dialogue. The first talkie vampire movie was Tod Browning's 1931 classic *Dracula*, which starred Bela Lugosi as the titular count.[139] This movie set the standard for all vampire films, and studios have remade it many times since then. Due to the story's immense popularity and widespread prevalence, it is unnecessary to delve into the storyline of Dracula.

Culturally, *Dracula* took society by storm. It was such a success that sequels and spinoffs were soon ordered. Further, Lugosi's eerie portrayal of the main character firmly cemented Dracula's status as a cultural icon. This film is so important that in 2000 it was preserved in the National Film Registry as "culturally, historically, or aesthetically significant."[140]

Other classic vampire movies from the 1930s include *The Vampire Bat* (1933) and *Mark of the Vampire* (1935). These movies featured the likes of Lugosi, Lionel Atwill, and Fay Wray as the female leads. It should be noted that while there were earlier shorts (short films) with vampiric titles, most had nothing to do with the legendary vampire. Additionally, earlier films featuring female "vampires" portrayed them as "vamps," or seductive and loose women. Vampire or vamp was simply a metaphor for seduction, mystery, and darkness.

---

138   [138] Ebert, Roger (28 September 1997). "Nosferatu Movie Review & Film Summary (1922)". RogerEbert.com.
139   [139] Skal, David J. (2004). Hollywood Gothic: The Tangled Web of Dracula from Novel to Stage to Screen, Paperback ed. New York: Faber & Faber.
140   [140] "Librarian of Congress Names 25 More Films to National Film Registry". Library of Congress.

The 1940s saw a shift in the portrayal of vampires as they moved away from being portrayed as monsters and instead became more romanticized figures. The most famous example of this was in the 1943 movie *The Vampire's Kiss*, starring John Carradine as the vampire.

The 1950s saw a resurgence of interest in horror movies, and vampires once again became a popular subject. Some of the most famous movies of the decade include *I Was a Teenage Vampire* (1957), *The Vampire* (1957), and *The Horror of Dracula* (1958).

The 1960s and 1970s saw a decline in vampire movies, but the genre made a comeback in the 1980s with the release of *The Lost Boys* (1987). This movie was a cult classic that helped to revitalize interest in vampires. The 1990s saw a wave of vampire movies thanks to the success of the *Twilight* franchise. The franchise spawned a number of spinoffs and sequels and revitalized the genre for the modern age.

The modern era of vampire movies has seen a wide variety of interpretations of the classic monster. From the campy comedy of *What We Do In The Shadows* (2014) to the dark and brooding atmosphere of *Let The Right One In* (2008), vampires have certainly come a long way since their inception in early cinema.

Video Games

Vampires have long been a staple of the horror genre, and as such, they have made their way into the realm of video games. From the classic *Castlevania* series to the more modern *Bloodborne* and *Vampyr*, vampires have been featured as both protagonists and antagonists in countless games. The *Castlevania* series is the most iconic vampire-themed video game series, having first been released on the Nintendo Entertainment System in 1986. The series follows the Belmont family as they battle against the powerful Count Dracula and his minions.[141] The series has spawned numerous sequels and

---

141   "Castlevania: A Dracula Masterpiece 90 Years in the Making". Den

spin-offs, including the recently released *Castlevania: Lords of Shadow*.

Bloodborne is a critically acclaimed action RPG developed by FromSoftware. Set in the gothic city of Yharnam, the game follows the player character as they battle against hordes of monsters, including vampires. Bloodborne features fast-paced combat and a unique world that draws heavily from H.P. Lovecraft's works. *Vampyr* is an action RPG developed by Dontnod Entertainment. Set in 1918 London, the game follows the player character, a recently turned vampire, as they battle against supernatural forces. The game features an intriguing morality system that rewards players for making choices that reflect their character's personality.

Finally, *Vampire: The Masquerade – Bloodlines* is an action role-playing game based on White Wolf's tabletop RPG. The game follows the player character as they explore the dark and gritty world of the *World of Darkness*. With an intriguing story and multiple endings, *Vampire: The Masquerade – Bloodlines* is an immersive and captivating game that remains a favorite of many fans. Vampires have become a staple of the horror genre, and as such, they have been featured in countless video games. Whether you are looking for fast-paced action, a tactical RPG, or an immersive story, there is sure to be a vampire-themed game for you.

The presence of vampires in video games demonstrates ways in which the folklore of these creatures has been successfully incorporated into a variety of settings and contexts. For example, while *Castlevania* evokes the classic themes of European folklore, *Vampire: The Masquerade – Bloodlines* is evocative of the modern New Orleans vampire tradition.[142] With each retelling and adaptation, the vampire myth lives on in modern technological storytelling.

---

of Geek!. Archived from the original on September 26, 2018.
142   Dillon, R., & Lundberg, A. (2017). Vampires in Video Games: Mythic Tropes for Innovative Storytelling. ETropic: Electronic Journal of Studies in the Tropics, 16(1).
https://doi.org/10.25120/etropic.16.1.2017.3578

Comics and Graphic Novels

Vampires have been a staple of comic books and graphic novels since the early days of the industry. From the classic horror comics of the Golden Age of Comics to the more contemporary supernatural stories of today, vampires have been a major part of the comic book landscape for decades. One of the earliest examples of vampires in comics was the iconic Count Dracula, who first appeared in Marvel's *Tomb of Dracula* in 1972.[143] This series, written by Marv Wolfman and drawn by Gene Colan, was one of the first to introduce a serious take on the vampire mythos. The series ran for seventy issues and spawned numerous spin-off titles, such *as The Tomb of Dracula Presents: The Curse of the Undead, Dracula Lives!*, and *Dracula: The Company of Monsters*.

In the modern era, vampires have become even more prevalent in comics. From the gothic horror of Dark Horse's *Hellboy* to the action-packed fantasy of Marvel's *Blade* to the darkly romantic *Vampire: The Masquerade* series, vampires have a wide variety of stories and genres to explore. In addition to traditional vampire stories, vampires have also been used as metaphors for other issues, such as teenage angst and the struggle between good and evil. For example, the popular manga series *Vampire Knight* explored themes of love, friendship, and morality, while the Vertigo series *American Vampire* explored themes of racism and identity.[144]

No matter their genre, vampires will always remain a popular part of the comic book and graphic novel world. Whether they are used as metaphors for real-world issues or simply as an entertaining source of horror, vampires will remain a staple of the comic book landscape for years to come.

---

143   [143] Sanderson, Peter (2008). "1970s". In Gilbert, Laura (ed.). Marvel Chronicle A Year-by-Year History. London, United Kingdom: Dorling Kindersley. p. 155.
144   Geddes, John (October 30, 2009). "Stephen King and Scott Snyder give Vampire an evolutionary twist". USA Today

The Runway

Vampires have been inspiring fashion trends for decades. The vampire's influence on fashion is undeniable; from gothic-inspired clothing to vampire-themed makeup, its influence is evident in today's fashion scene. From the romantic gothic looks of the Victorian era to the edgy and modern styles of today, vampires have a long-lasting influence on fashion. In the Victorian era, vampires were seen as romantic figures, and so their influence was manifested in the fashion of the time. Women's clothing was often designed with a high neckline, long sleeves, and a long skirt that reached the ground, which was meant to cover the body and create a sense of mystery. Men's clothing was also designed with a high neckline and long sleeves, but they were often more fitted and tailored.

The vampire influence in fashion from this time was also seen in the fabrics used. Dark velvet materials in black, red, and purple shades were popular for both men and women. Lace and frills were also often used to add a romantic touch to the look.[145] In modern times, the vampire influence on fashion is seen in the trend of wearing black. One such aspect can be seen in the minimalist black outfits that many people wear today. It is also seen in the popularity of leather jackets and boots, which have been seen in vampire-inspired films and television shows.

Vampire influence can also be recognized in the popular makeup and hairstyles today. Dark eyeshadows and lipsticks are often used to create a vampire-like look, and red and black hair colors are popular. Vampire culture has had a lasting influence on fashion throughout the years, and it continues to inspire modern trends. Whether you are looking for a romantic gothic look or a more edgy and modern style, you can find something to fit your vampire-inspired fashion needs.

---

145   [145] Pérez Zurutuza, Kristian, Images of Diluted Masculinity of Contemporary Vampire Characters through Racial Discourse in Modern American Gothic (April 1, 2016). IJAS - International Journal of Arts & Sciences - ISSN: 1944-6934, Vol. 09(02), p. 335–356, 2016, Available at SSRN: https://ssrn.com/abstract=2960706

Music

The vampire has been a source of inspiration for music and art for centuries, and its influence can be seen in a variety of genres. From classical music to modern pop culture, the vampire has had a profound effect on music and art. The vampire remains a prevalent subject in art and music today. From the darkly romantic tones of gothic rock to the edgy style of metal, the vampire has had a hand in shaping many musical genres. Even more recently, vampires have been featured prominently in rap and hip-hop, with songs such as Drake's *"God's Plan"* giving a nod to vampire lore. It is clear that the vampire has had an immense impact on the music industry, and it shows no signs of waning anytime soon.

Classical Music

It may be surprising to learn that the vampire has been a source of inspiration for classical composers for centuries. Since classical music's earliest days, composers have used the vampire to evoke a sense of dread and mystery.[146] The vampire's dark and mysterious nature has been used to create a wide range of musical styles, from the eerie, romantic music of composers like Franz Liszt to the gothic soundscapes of modern composers like Gustav Mahler.

The music of the vampire is an ever-evolving art form, often reflecting the cultural anxieties and conditions of its time. For example, the works of composers like Stravinsky and Mussorgsky tapped into themes of death and darkness that mirrored the mood of the late 19th century. Similarly, 20th-century composers captured a modern, psychological sense of dread in their scores for horror films.[147] Today's modern

---

146   [146] Chamberlain, S., & Chamberlain, S. (2017, October 1). Classical Music's Vampires: An October playlist. Mask of the Flower Prince. https://maskoftheflowerprince.wordpress.com/2017/10/01/classical-musics-vampires-an-october-playlist/#:~:text=Vampires%20have%20been%20a%20staple,%2C%20poetry%2C%20and%20religious%20treatises.

147   [147] Interlude. (2019, November 22). Classical music inspired by

composers continue to explore the vampire's musical possibilities with unique styles and interpretations.

Pop Music

The vampire has had a major impact on pop music as well. From the iconic *"Thriller"* by Michael Jackson to the recent hit song *"Vampire Weekend"* by Vampire Weekend, the vampire has been used to create a wide range of musical styles. Vampire-themed songs often feature themes of loneliness, death, and loss while also exploring the dark and mysterious side of the vampire.

The vampire's influence on music can be heard in the lyrics of many popular songs. For example, The Killers' hit song *"The Vampire"* explores themes of love and death. Other songs like *"Dracula's Wedding"* by Outkast and *"Vampire in Brooklyn"* by Rihanna have also been popular. All these songs embrace the mysterious and dark aspects of the vampire while still being incredibly catchy and appealing to listeners. Perhaps this is why the vampire has become such an iconic figure in the world of music.

Rock Music

Not only has the vampire archetype played a role in influencing pop music, it has greatly shaped rock music as well. From the early days of rock and roll with bands like The Rolling Stones and Led Zeppelin to modern bands like My Chemical Romance and 30 Seconds to Mars, the vampire has been used to create a wide range of musical styles. Vampire themes have been used to create a sense of tension and suspense, as well as explore topics of darkness and mystery.

Vampires have additionally been used to explore the idea of love and romance. As the living dead, vampires embody a unique combination of human emotions and inhuman powers. Bands such as Evanescence and The Cure have used the

---

Dracula. Interlude. https://interlude.hk/inspiration-imagination-dracula/

vampire to symbolize forbidden love and passion, while others like The Misfits and Type O Negative have explored violence and death in their music. Many modern bands are also using vampire themes to explore more nuanced topics, such as identity and self-expression.

Art

Vampire themes have posed an incredible influence on art as well. From the gothic paintings of the 19th century to modern art, the vampire has been used to create a wide range of art styles. The vampire has inspired a wide breadth of art styles, from the romantic paintings of the Pre-Raphaelites to the dark and surreal works of contemporary artists like Damien Hirst. The vampire's influence on art is undeniable. Like with music, its dark and mysterious nature has been used to create a wide range of artistic styles, from classical music to modern pop culture. The vampire has been used to evoke a sense of dread and mystery and explore themes of loneliness, death, and loss. Its influence on art will continue to be felt for centuries to come.

Edvard Munch debuted his masterpiece *The Vampire* in 1893. Originally titled *Love and Pain*, the painting depicts a woman sitting bent over a man resting his head in her lap. He released a series of such paintings with similar motifs.[148] In one, the woman was kissing the man on the neck. Or was she perhaps biting?

Similarly, the piece *Dante and Virgil* (1859) by William Bouguereau features two men locked in battle, with one biting the other's neck while Dante and his guide Virgil navigate the perils of Hell.[149] Furthermore, a bat-winged demon is hovering over the scene, reminiscent of the bats, which vampires are said to morph into. While based upon The Divine Comedy, the

---

148 [148] Google. (n.d.). Vampire - Edvard Munch - Google Arts & Culture. Google. https://artsandculture.google.com/asset/vampire-edvard-munch/MwFWVPAFcZrcfQ?hl=en

149 [149] "Musée d'Orsay: William Bouguereau Dante and Virgil". musee-orsay.fr.

artwork presents many of the themes intrinsic to vampire mythos, such as the concept of eternal damnation.

From literature to television, the vampire remains prevalent in popular culture. Count Dracula, for example, continues to be featured in many films, books, and television series. The vampire's influence on popular culture is so strong that it symbolizes society's macabre and supernatural aspects. Even today, vampires are still seen as mysterious creatures of the night and a source of fascination for many people.

What is Society's Fascination with the Vampire?

The vampire, as a figure of myth and legend, captivated audiences for centuries. This enduring fascination has been reignited in modern society, with the vampire emerging as one of the most common figures in pop culture. From literature and film to television and video games, the vampire has become an iconic symbol of modern society. It is a powerful symbol of the modern world, representing some of the darker aspects of humanity. This includes a fascination with death and mortality and a more sinister allure of power and control. In literature, vampires often challenge traditional social norms and taboos, allowing readers to explore their inner desires and fears. In film, vampires can provide a thrilling escape from reality while also providing a window to explore the darker side of human nature.

The vampire further represents modern culture, demonstrating themes of sexuality, power, and social status. This is particularly reflected in the *Twilight* and *Vampire Diaries* franchises, which have become wildly popular in recent years. These stories provide a form of escapism for fans, allowing them to explore these themes in a safe and entertaining way. The vampire has become an important part of modern society because it allows people to explore and express their feelings and desires safely and creatively. It also provides an opportunity to explore the darker aspects of human nature, which can often be difficult to discuss in traditional settings. Finally, it provides a way for people to connect with each other around a common interest, allowing them to share their thoughts, feelings, and experiences.

Chapter 11 The Modern Vampire

Modern vampires are a far cry from the traditional vampires of folklore and literature. Nowadays, vampires are often depicted as attractive, sensitive, and even heroic characters in supernatural fiction, television series, and films. The modern vampire is usually portrayed as a complex being, often with a tortured soul. They may lead a double life, struggling to balance the need to sustain themselves on human blood while trying to remain a moral, upstanding member of society. They often have supernatural powers such as superhuman strength and speed, the ability to transform into a bat or wolf, and the ability to mesmerize and control humans.

Unlike the classic vampires of old, modern vampires are often seen as victims of their own nature, cursed with an insatiable thirst for blood. They may be portrayed as romantic figures using their powers to protect humans from other supernatural creatures. Modern vampires also often have a fashion sense to match their immortal status. They are often dressed in stylish, gothic clothing, accessorized with capes and jewelry. They may even embrace the vampire lifestyle and become part of a vampire subculture, attending Goth clubs and social events.

Modern vampires are a far cry from the traditional monsters of myth and legend. They are complex creatures struggling with their own inner demons while trying to fit in with the human world. Whether they are a force of evil or a force of good, they remain an intriguing part of our cultural landscape.

Subculture

Modern Vampire subculture is a growing community of people who are fascinated by vampires, the supernatural, and the power of the night.[150] It has been around since at least the late 1990s and has grown to become one of the most popular

---

150   [150] Browning, J. The real vampires of New Orleans and Buffalo: a research note towards comparative ethnography. Palgrave Commun 1, 15006 (2015). https://doi.org/10.1057/palcomms.2015.6

subcultures in the world. People who are part of the modern vampire subculture may identify as "real vampires," and they may practice certain rituals or lifestyle choices to express their beliefs. These include drinking blood, wearing dark clothing, and embracing the idea of immortality.[151] They also often participate in vampire-themed parties and events or even engage in vampire role-playing games.

This subculture has stemmed from the so-called goth subculture.[152] The goth subculture began in the 1980s in the UK and centered around fans of goth music, which in itself was an offshoot of post-punk genre music. As can be easily imagined, the goth subculture is additionally influenced by 19th-century gothic fiction and early 20th-century horror movies. Furthermore, this subculture drew inspiration from early mythologies such as Celtic, Egyptian, and Paganism.[153] It would appear that the vampire subculture would be a natural progression or off shoot of the goth subculture.

The modern vampire subculture has been made popular by books and movies such as Twilight, True Blood, and even the classic Dracula. It is also common to find people who identify as modern vampires on social media, often engaging in conversations and activities related to the subculture. Many people have embraced the modern vampire lifestyle, or subculture, and find it to be a way to express their beliefs and connect with others who share their interests. It is a unique and often misunderstood subculture, but it has become an accepted part of the modern world.

Within this style of subculture, there exist numerous variations of lifestyle. For example, there are those who identify as "Sanguinarians" or those who consume the blood of

---

151   [151] Mellins, Maria (2013). "Vampire Community Profile". Vampire Culture. Dress, Body, Culture. London: Bloomsbury Academic. pp. 45–68.
152   Skal, David J. (1993). The Monster Show: A Cultural History of Horror. New York: Penguin. pp. 342–43.
153   [153] Goodlad, Lauren M. E.; Bibby, Michael (2007). "Introduction". In Goodlad, Lauren M. E.; Bibby, Michael (eds.). Goth: Undead Subculture. Durham, North Carolina: Duke University Press. pp. 1–37.

others. Meanwhile, others identify as "Psychic Vampires." They feed upon the aura or energy field of others.[154] As one can see, the vampire subculture is varied and offers numerous ways of self-expression which will be further addressed in this chapter.

Safe Houses

A modern vampire safehouse is a secure space where vampires can congregate and hide away from humans. Such safe houses are often set up in the shadows of cities or in remote rural areas. Inside, vampires can find all the comforts of home, including beds, bathrooms, and kitchens. Many of these safe houses also feature blood banks, allowing vampires to feed without having to hunt. Some even contain libraries, allowing vampires to learn more about their kind and the world at large.

The Atlanta Vampire Alliance's mission statement is *"to promote unity in the greater Atlanta, Georgia, real Vampire Community while being available to the newly awakened to encourage self-awareness and responsibility. We honor the traditions of history, respect, and discretion regarding Community affairs while advocating for the safety and well-being of our members. Emphasizing research and support of social gatherings, we highlight the importance of education and the strength of involvement as a cohesive force in our area. By taking an active role, we will serve not only ourselves but also our Community and our City."*[155]

In addition to providing a safe haven for vampires, modern vampire safehouses also feature plenty of modern amenities. These can include computers, high-speed internet access, televisions, gaming systems, and more. This allows vampires to stay connected to the outside world and to communicate with one another. Finally, modern vampire safehouses are equipped

---

[154] Keyworth, David (October 2002). "The Socio-Religious Beliefs and Nature of the Contemporary Vampire Subculture." Journal of Contemporary Religion. 17 (3): 355–370.
[155] A Real Vampire House. Atlanta Vampire Alliance [AVA]. (n.d.-a). http://www.atlantavampirealliance.com/missionfaq.html

with state-of-the-art security systems. This ensures that vampires remain safe and protected from any potential threats. Special wards and spells can also be used to help shield the safehouse and its inhabitants from human detection.

Modern vampire safehouses provide vampires with a safe and comfortable place to rest, feed, and stay connected to the world. These safehouses provide a haven for vampires to live and thrive by providing a secure environment and the modern amenities that vampires need.

Feeding Techniques for the Sanguinarians

Modern Sanguinarian vampires have developed feeding techniques that are much more discreet and sophisticated than those used by their predecessors. Instead of biting into their victims' necks, modern vampires focus on feeding from extremities such as the wrists, ankles, and inner elbows. This technique allows the vampire to feed from the same area multiple times without leaving any visible marks.

Vampires also use a technique called 'venom feeding.' This involves the vampire piercing their victim's skin with a tooth and injecting numbing venom that inhibits pain. This venom also has a sedative effect and can cause the victim to become complacent and compliant. The consumption of blood from human sources is facilitated through a consensual agreement by a verbal or written contract between the vampire and the donor. Most use an official Donor Bill of Rights. For example, the transcript used by the New Orleans Vampire Association makes it quite clear that this blood exchange is a mutual agreement, and at any time, the donor is free to decline.[156]

Furthermore, it should be noted that the majority of blood feeding is done in a hygienic manner utilizing modern medical implements as well as laboratory blood testing. Such measures ensure the safety of both the vampire and the donor. Each

---

156   [156] Ashantison, B. (n.d.). Donor Bill of Rights. New Orleans Vampire Association. http://www.neworleansvampireassociation.org/donor-bill-of-rights.html

vampire has their own preferred method of feeding. One report detailed a session in which a small scalpel was used on the donor's back to draw a small amount of blood. The vampire then sucked the blood from the small wound and afterward cleaned it for the donor.[157] This is a far cry from the old legends of taking blood by force from a wound in the neck. However, blood drinking isn't the only way for modern vampires to feed.

Introduction to Modern Psychic Vampires

Modern vampires also feed off energy instead of physical blood. This is achieved through 'psychic feeding,' where vampire uses their mental powers to draw energy from their victims. This energy replenishes the vampire's strength and vitality, allowing them to remain active and alive. Modern psychic vampires are people who drain the energy of other people in order to satisfy their own needs.[158] This is accomplished by using their own psychic energy to absorb other people's energy. Psychic vampires do this in a variety of ways, including telepathy, energy manipulation, and emotional manipulation. Psychic vampires exist in the modern world, though their exact numbers are unknown.

The term "psychic vampire" first appeared in the mid-1980s and has become increasingly popular in recent years. Psychic vampires are often associated with the occult, though some people believe they can also be found in everyday life. Psychic vampires are believed to be able to have the ability to manipulate emotions, thoughts, and even physical sensations. These abilities are further believed to be linked to their power to absorb energy from other people. This form of energy theft often leaves the victim feeling drained, exhausted, and even sick.

---

157   [157] Wang, Y. (2021, October 25). Inside the Human Blood-drinking, "Real Vampire" Community of New Orleans. The Washington Post. https://www.washingtonpost.com/news/morning-mix/wp/2015/10/26/inside-the-human-blood-drinking-real-vampire-community-of-new-orleans/
158   Frost, Brian J. (1989). The monster with a thousand faces: guises of the vampire in myth and literature. Popular Press.

In some cases, psychic vampires may be able to sense the thoughts and emotions of other people. This is known as "empathic sensing" and is thought to be a form of telepathy. This ability allows them to gain insight into the thoughts and feelings of other people and can be used to manipulate and control them. It is important to note that psychic vampires are not necessarily evil or malicious. Many people believe they can be helpful and provide guidance and healing to those in need.

The most dangerous type of modern energy vampire is the spiritual vampire. This type of vampire will drain the victim's spiritual energy, leaving them feeling spiritually, emotionally, and physically drained. This type of vampire is particularly dangerous because it can affect the victim's mental and emotional state, leaving them feeling depressed, anxious, and overwhelmed. It is important to recognize that some psychic vampires may engage in manipulative and harmful behaviors, which should be avoided when possible.

Modern Emotional and Physical Vampires

The most common type of modern energy vampire is the emotional vampire. These individuals often seek out those who are vulnerable and emotionally needy. They will use manipulation and persuasion to get what they want, often leaving the victim feeling drained, confused, and helpless. Such forms of vampirism are considered toxic and are often treated as an observed mental condition based upon victim testimonies. Emotional vampires utilize a plethora of emotionally controlling techniques against their victims, draining them of their emotional energy.[159]

Physical energy vampires also exist. These individuals will drain their victim's energy through physical contact, often through sex. However, it may also be accomplished through simple hugging and kissing. Again, this type of vampire leaves the victim feeling drained and exhausted. This feeling is quite

---

159   Bernstein, A. J. (2012). Emotional vampires: Dealing with people who drain you dry. McGraw-Hill.

different from a pleasant exhaustion after lovemaking. The victim traditionally will feel empty inside, as if the coupling had created a void. It isn't unusual for sexual vampires to feed and then never contact their victims again.[160]

No matter what type of modern energy vampire you may encounter, taking steps to protect yourself is important. Stay aware of your surroundings and maintain healthy boundaries. It is also important to take care of yourself physically and emotionally. Taking care of yourself will help you better protect yourself from modern energy vampires.

The Vampire Lifestyle

Another modern form of vampirism is simply adopting a vampire lifestyle without the aspect of feeding on others. These sorts of vampires are often called role-players and readily acknowledge that they are assuming the role of a vampire.[161] It is common for those participating in this subculture to dress in a vampire style of clothing and restrict their outings to the nighttime hours.

Those who consider themselves real vampires prefer not to be associated with lifestylers, yet they accept their lifestyle counterparts readily. Lifestylers, those who embrace the vampire lifestyle, welcome the vampiric folkloric elements into their world. They adopt not only gothic fashion but also the mannerisms of the vampire.[162] Additionally, they participate in their own events, gatherings, and parties.

Lifestylers have been known to form their own communities in order to share their beliefs and experiences. They may also

---

160   Llewellyn Worldwide, Ltd. (2004, February 9). Emotional and Sexual Vampires. Llewellyn Worldwide. https://www.llewellyn.com/journal/article/561#:~:text=Sexual%20vampires%20are%20those%20people,as%20if%20they%20were%20disposable.
161   [161] Browning, J. The real vampires of New Orleans and Buffalo: a research note towards comparative ethnography. Palgrave Commun 1, 15006 (2015). https://doi.org/10.1057/palcomms.2015.6
162   [162] Black Veil Vampire FAQ. BlackVeilVampires.com. (n.d.). http://www.blackveilvampires.com/faq

partake in activities such as roleplaying, meditation, and spirituality. Despite the differences between real vampires and lifestylers, many of them are still able to come together in a respectful and accepting environment. Furthermore, lifestylers are often open to learning about the real vampires' practices and rituals, allowing for an interesting exchange of knowledge.

Exploring the Appeal of Becoming a Modern Vampire

Vampires have been popular figures in folklore and popular culture for centuries, but in recent years, more and more people are choosing to self-identify as modern vampires. These modern vampires are often people who feel a connection to vampire mythos and seek to embody the power and mystique associated with the creature. So, why do people choose to become modern vampires? There are a variety of reasons, but some of the most commonly cited are the feeling of immortality, the power and strength of being a vampire, and the sense of community within the vampire subculture.

For many people, the idea of immortality is an attractive one. However, becoming a vampire does not grant them a kind of eternal life that many humans cannot experience, but it allows them to become strong and unique individuals. As a modern vampire, they can live a life aligned with their ideals. Additionally, there is an appeal to the power and strength associated with the vampire archetype. Many people are drawn to the idea of having strength and power beyond what is possible for a human being. They may also enjoy the idea of being feared and respected by those who know their identity.

Finally, the sense of community within the vampire subculture is another reason people may choose to become modern vampires. By joining the vampire lifestyle, individuals can find a place where they feel accepted and appreciated for who they are without fear of judgment or ridicule. People can also make friends and allies within the community and share experiences and knowledge about the vampire lifestyle. Overall, the decision to become a modern vampire is personal and varies from individual to individual. Ultimately, it is up to each person to decide if the vampire lifestyle is right for them.

Chapter 12: Ailments

Vampirism has been the subject of many stories and legends throughout the centuries, but what is the actual cause of this mysterious condition? A number of ailments have been suggested over the years to explain vampirism. While none of these can be definitively proven, they offer interesting possibilities for why some people might exhibit unusual behaviors and traits associated with vampirism.

While none of these ailments definitively explain the cause of vampirism, they offer interesting possibilities for why some people might exhibit behaviors and traits associated with the condition. Ultimately, the answer to the mystery of vampirism remains unknown. Despite the lack of a definitive answer, it is clear that vampires have played an important role in folklore and storytelling for centuries. The figure of the vampire has been used to represent fear, danger, seduction, and even redemption in popular culture. As such, it is not surprising that so many people are fascinated by vampires and their mysterious origins. It is likely that the debate surrounding vampirism will continue for many years to come.

Sleep disorders

Sleep disorders, such as insomnia and narcolepsy, can lead to a range of physical and mental symptoms, such as lethargy, irritability, and an aversion to sunlight. These symptoms could explain the vampire's need to sleep during the day and their heightened sensitivity to sunlight. A recent academic study attributed Trauma-Associated Sleep Disorder (TSD) as a possible explanation behind the vampire phenomena. For example, in Bram Stoker's titular novel *Dracula*, when Mina declines to join Van Helsing in confronting the vampire, the novel states, "even if she be not harmed...she may suffer--both in waking, from her nerves and in sleep, from her dreams."[163] Researchers believed that by this, Stoker implied that without

---

163   [163] Stoker B. Drácula 1897. Bram Stoker; 2014.

physical injury, the distress caused by the trauma poses severe psychological distress, which may manifest itself while the victim is sleeping.[164] It's quite convenient as vampires tend to only strike at night.

The researchers go on to remark that there exists a number of Disruptive Nocturnal Behaviors (DNB) after a traumatic event, such as nightmares and insomnia. Taking this theory a step further, within the context of vampirism, a severe and undiagnosed or untreated case of insomnia would cause a person to not only be more active at night, but numerous studies point to behavioral changes as well with sleep deprivation. Furthermore, consider the physical appearance of one who suffers such sleep disturbances. Such a person would naturally be rather pale with dark circles under their eyes.

Additionally, vampires have difficulty controlling their emotions and behaviors, which can also be attributed to the effects of sleep deprivation. The violent reenactment of dreams, while reported centuries ago, was not formally diagnosed until the 1980s.[165] To someone unaccustomed to such a disorder, it would look as though the victim were fighting an invisible force or attacker. It must be taken into consideration the key demographic of those who suffer from such conditions. Typically, they are men below the age of forty years old with a military history of combat.[166] A cursory glance at a history book reveals the terrible truth that our world has a nasty habit of continual battle. Furthermore, pandemics must be taken into consideration and the psychological effects that they bring with

---

164 [164] Rachakonda TD, Balba NM, Lim MM. Trauma-Associated Sleep Disturbances: a Distinct Sleep Disorder? Curr Sleep Med Rep. 2018 Jun;4(2):143-148. doi: 10.1007/s40675-018-0119-2. Epub 2018 Apr 26. PMID: 30656131; PMCID: PMC6330699.
165 [165] Schenck CH, Bundlie SR, Ettinger MG, Mahowald MW. Chronic behavioral disorders of human REM sleep: a new category of parasomnia. Sleep. 1986;9(2):293–308.
166 [166] Hefez A, Metz L, Lavie P. Long-term effects of extreme situational stress on sleep and dreaming. The American journal of psychiatry. 1987

the rampant illness and death. How might these situations shape the psychological terrain of the dreamscape?

Tuberculosis

Earlier in this book, the New England Vampire Panic was discussed. The panic resulted from the rampant spread of tuberculosis or TB. In the 19th century, tuberculosis was called Galloping Consumption because it was quickly and easily spread, and the disease seemed to literally consume the patient. In cases of TB, the disease is caused by bacteria that attack the lungs.[167] Due to the pale skin tone of affected patients, it was also called the Great White Plague, and no one was safe from its effects. Further, as the disease attacks the lungs, coughing fits ensue as lung tissue is destroyed. As a result, patients commonly cough up blood. This, combined with their pale countenance, one could assume them to be vampires.

Furthermore, during the 19th century, modern society was in an industrial age, and conditions were not only cramped, but they were also not as sanitary as they should have been. As a result, TB spread rapidly within this environment. Combine this with early folk belief in vampires, and it is unsurprising that a vampire panic ensued in New England during this time.[168]

Sensory Processing Disorder

Sensory Processing Disorder is a neurological disorder which can cause difficulty processing certain sensory information, such as sounds and smells.[169] This could explain the vampire's

---

167 [167] Editorial Staff, How We Conquuered Consumption, The American Lung Association, https://www.lung.org/blog/how-we-conquered-consumption
168 [168] Sledzik PS, Bellantoni N. Brief communication: bioarcheological and biocultural evidence for the New England vampire folk belief. Am J Phys Anthropol. 1994 Jun;94(2):269-74. doi: 10.1002/ajpa.1330940210. PMID: 8085617.
169 [169] Miller LJ, Nielsen DM, Schoen SA, Brett-Green BA. Perspectives on sensory processing disorder: a call for translational research. Front Integr Neurosci. 2009 Sep 30;3:22. doi: 10.3389/neuro.07.022.2009. PMID: 19826493; PMCID: PMC2759332.

heightened sense of smell and hearing, as well as their aversion to garlic and other strong odors. Additionally, those with SPD may also feel an aversion to sunlight as it is simply too bright. With SPD, patients can become overwhelmed by the incoming sensory information and, in turn, react strongly or perhaps even lash out. Consider a vampire running to the shade when confronted by sunlight.

Today, Sensory Processing Disorder, while very real to experiencers, is not an officially recognized medical diagnosis. As with many new psychological findings, SPD is currently recognized most easily in children, as adults with the disorder tend to mask it well. Interestingly, those with SPD, it has been discovered, often withdraw and self-isolate.[170] Much like a vampire who can't tolerate loud noises, strong smells, and sunlight may choose to live life away from society.

Conversely, SPD can also present as sensory seeking instead of sensory avoiding.[171] This can cause a person to act impulsively or present in other ways, such as sensorimotor issues. Sensorimotor issues include the way in which a person may walk. Imagine Nosferatu of the early cinema. Sensory seeking may also lead one to choose pleasing tactile style fabrics such as velvet. SPD has been linked to neurodivergent brain chemistry, anxiety, and food intolerance.[172] Within the context of pre-modern vampirism, it is easy to see similarities to such behaviors displayed in SPD and one being neurodivergent or having a food intolerance. For example, what everyone else eats makes a person with a food intolerance quite

---

170   [170] Staff, Familydoctor. org E. (2023, May 15). Sensory Processing Disorder (SPD). familydoctor.org. https://familydoctor.org/condition/sensory-processing-disorder-spd/
171   Peters SU, Horowitz L, Barbieri-Welge R, Taylor JL, Hundley RJ (February 2012). "Longitudinal follow-up of autism spectrum features and sensory behaviors in Angelman syndrome by deletion class". Journal of Child Psychology and Psychiatry, and Allied Disciplines. 53 (2): 152–9.
172   Lane AE, Young RL, Baker AE, Angley MT (January 2010). "Sensory processing subtypes in autism: association with adaptive behavior". Journal of Autism and Developmental Disorders. 40 (1): 112–22.

ill. Furthermore, what may seem normal to those who are neurotypical (typical brain chemistry) may be extreme for those who are neurodivergent (autistic/ADHD). Before such behaviors were understood, anyone outside of the "norm" could be considered a vampire due to these conditions.

Mental Illness

Mental illness, such as depression and anxiety, can cause a range of symptoms, such as social isolation, nightmares, and an increased interest in the supernatural. This could explain why some people believe themselves to be vampires and why they might exhibit certain behaviors associated with vampirism. Schizophrenia and Paraphilia both have been causes behind what is now dubbed clinical vampirism.[173]

Clinical vampirism, more commonly known as Renfield's syndrome, is an obsession with drinking blood. The earliest presentation of clinical vampirism in psychiatric literature was a psychoanalytic interpretation of two cases, contributed by Richard L. Vanden Bergh and John. F. Kelley.[174] It must be noted that clinically, less than 100 cases have been reported of Clinical vampirism.

One such case involved a patient in her late 30s. She had experienced vampiristic fantasies during puberty yet had never acted upon them. However, she sustained a traumatic brain injury while in the military at the age of 23, which resulted in three weeks of unconsciousness. Upon gaining consciousness, her behavior began to shift as an insatiable blood lust took hold. It was at this point that she began to engage in self-harm, such as cutting, in order to drink her own blood.[175]

---

173 [173] Jensen, HM; Poulsen, HD (2002). "Auto-vampirism in schizophrenia". Nordic Journal of Psychiatry. 56 (1): 47–48.
174 Vanden Bergh, Richard L.; Kelley, John F. (1964). "Vampirism -- A review with new observations". Archives of General Psychiatry. 11: 543–547.
175 [175]Hervey WM, Catalano G, Catalano MC. Vampiristic behaviors in a patient with traumatic brain injury-induced disinhibition. World J Clin Cases. 2016 Jun 16;4(6):138-41. doi: 10.12998/wjcc.v4.i6.138. PMID:

In her 30s, she sought medical and psychiatric help. It was then discovered that the patient did not suffer from any form of depressive or anxious mental state resulting in her self-harm. Interestingly, during scans, it was revealed that her frontal cortex had sustained damage from her earlier injury. She was diagnosed as fitting the category of autovampirism[176] and the subcategory of self-induced bleeding and ingestion of blood.[177] Medical professionals regard the traumatic brain injury as the defining characteristic of this patient's disorder, as it caused her inhibitions about vampiristic fantasies to be unconstrained.

Rabies and Porphyria

Modern scientists have proposed a number of theories as to the medical background of supposed vampirism. UCLA historian Paul Barber wrote in the Journal of Folklore Research that vampire stories are not simple horror stories but are clever folk-hypothesis that attempt to explain puzzling occurrences linked to death and decomposition.[178] Conversely, Dr. Gomez-Alonso remarks that in some cases, rabies may appear similar to vampirism. He goes on to say that a rabid patient may rush at those who approach him, biting them like he were a wild beast. In both cases, the method of transmission is identical, caused by bites or blood-to-blood contact.[179] Today, dogs are the most commonly associated with rabies. However, rural villagers historically had much more interaction with wolves, which were a considerable threat both to themselves and their livestock.

27326398; PMCID: PMC4909458.
176 [176] Auto-vampirism is a form of vampirism that refers to drinking one's own blood.
177 [177] Prins H. Vampirism--legendary or clinical phenomenon? Med Sci Law. 1984;24:283–293.
178 BARBER, P. (2010). Vampires, Burial, and Death: Folklore and Reality. Yale University Press. http://www.jstor.org/stable/j.ctt1nq6gm
179 [179] Gómez-Alonso J. Rabies: a possible explanation for the vampire legend. Neurology. 1998 Sep;51(3):856-9. doi: 10.1212/wnl.51.3.856. PMID: 9748039.

Another theory is Porphyria Cutanea Tarda (PCT). PCT is a type of blood disorder which affects the skin. It is one of the most common types of porphyria and has been referred to as vampire disease. PCT is a disease which still affects people today. However, before the symptoms were understood, people often invented supernatural explanations for them.

Porphyria is a collective term for a group of disorders which are largely inherited. These disorders can be broadly classified into two categories: acute porphyrias, which predominantly affect the nervous system, and cutaneous porphyrias, which affects the skin. The primary issue in all types of porphyria is a disruption in the process that produces heme, a vital component of hemoglobin in the blood. Hemoglobin is present in red blood cells and facilitates the transportation of oxygen from the lungs to the body tissues during respiration. The accumulation of porphyrins in the body is a result of the disruption of heme production.

It has been suggested that there are four main connections between porphyria symptoms and vampire folklore. Firstly, the notion that vampires drink blood may have been derived from the fact that porphyria can cause red or brown urine. Professor Michael Hefferson of Queen's University has noted in a blog post that, prior to modern treatments for porphyria, some physicians had recommended that patients drink animal blood in order to compensate for the defect in their red blood cells.[180] This may have contributed to the superstition surrounding blood-drinking creatures of the night.

The famed sun-aversion of vampires is likely linked to the symptoms of PCT. People with PCT typically need to avoid the sun, as it can cause painful blistering, burning, and even permanent skin damage. This symptom would have been seen as strange to those living centuries ago; thus, it is unsurprising

---

180   Hefferon, M. (2020, June 29). Vampire Myths Originated with a Real Blood Disorder. Queen's Gazette | Queen's University. https://www.queensu.ca/gazette/stories/vampire-myths-originated-real-blood-disorder

that porphyria's extreme sun sensitivity became associated with vampire mythology.

Finally, the thought that vampires have fangs and are averse to garlic (or that garlic will harm them) may also have their origins in the symptoms of porphyria. Prolonged porphyria attacks can lead to facial disfigurement and can cause the gums to recede, resulting in a "fanged" appearance. As for garlic, it has a high sulfur content, which can act as a potential attack trigger for those with acute forms of porphyria.

Medical Misunderstandings?

Throughout the centuries, vampirism has been the subject of numerous tales and legends; however, the true cause of this enigmatic condition has yet to be identified. A variety of ailments have been suggested as potential explanations for vampirism, though none of these can be confirmed. Despite this, these theories offer intriguing potential explanations for why certain individuals may exhibit behaviors and attributes associated with vampirism. It is clear that vampires have maintained a prominent position in folklore and storytelling for many years. The vampire figure has been used to symbolize fear, peril, seduction, and even redemption in popular culture, which explains why so many people are captivated by vampires and their mysterious origins. It is probable that the debate regarding vampirism will continue for ages to come.

Chapter 13: The Hunters

Throughout the centuries, vampire hunters have been the stuff of legend and lore. From the ancient Greeks to the present day, tales of these hunters have been passed down through generations, each one with their own unique methods and motivations. Professional or semi-professional vampire hunters have been known to play a part in the vampire beliefs of the Balkans, particularly in Bulgarian, Serbian, and Romanian folk beliefs.

In Bulgarian, the terms used to refer to these hunters include glog (lit. "hawthorn," the species of wood used for the stake), vampirdzhiya, vampirar, dzhadazhiya, and svetocher. It was believed that those born on a Saturday (Sabbatarians, Bulgarian sâbotnichav, Greek sabbatianoí) or the offspring of a vampire and a woman (typically his widow, known as a dhampir in Romani or a vampirović in Serbian) could see a vampire when it was otherwise invisible.[181] Furthermore, it was believed that these Sabbatarians needed to be fed meat from a sheep killed by a wolf (Bulgarian vâlkoedene) to enable them not to fear the supernatural entities they were able to see. In Croatian and Slovenian legends, the villages had their own vampire hunters, called kresniks, whose spirits were able to turn into animals at night to fight off the vampire or kudlak.[182]

In the Middle Ages, vampire hunters were often members of the clergy, such as priests and monks. They would often use crucifixes and holy water to ward off vampires, as well as using incantations and prayers. Sometimes, these hunters would also use garlic, mirrors, and garlic-soaked stakes to pin the vampire to the ground. In the 19th century, vampire hunters began to take on a more scientific approach, observing and documenting the habits of vampires and attempting to uncover the secrets

---

181   [181] GF Abbott, Macedonian Folklore. Nature 69, 125 (1903). https://doi.org/10.1038/069125a0
182   Perkowski, Jan L. (1989). The Darkling: A Treatise on Slavic Vampirism. Columbus, Ohio: Slavica Publishers. pp. 31–32.

behind their power. They studied their victims, looking for any physical signs of a vampire attack.

The 21st century has seen a rise in the popularity of vampire hunters, with many books, films, and television shows centered around them. Though the methods used may have changed over the centuries, one thing remains the same: vampire hunters have always been brave individuals willing to go to extreme lengths in order to protect humanity.

First Vampire Hunter

Throughout the years, the figure of the vampire hunter has been a source of inspiration for literary and audiovisual works on both the small and big screen. Examples of these hunters of the "undead" can be seen in the television series Buffy and the character of Dr. Van Helsing in Dracula. However, to find the first documented vampire hunter or slayer, it is necessary to look to the Far East. Japan, to be exact.

Minamoto no Raiko was a samurai who lived from 948-1021. His legends are larger than life and continue to be shared today. He is famed for being an accomplished demon killer. One such legend is his triumph over the legendary Shutendoji. Shutendoji was a giant ogre who feasted upon the flesh of humans.[183] Minamoto no Raiko and his band of demon slayers disguised themselves as yamabushi, Japanese mountain hermits, and asked for shelter during the night.

While there, the Shutendoji offered the group human flesh, which they pretended to enjoy. After gaining the trust of the ogre, Minamoto poisoned him with a drugged wine, causing the monster to fall fast asleep. The group of warriors then tied up the vampire-like monster and beheaded him. However, the head jumped up of its own accord and bit into Raiko's helmet. Raiko, though, wore a solid golden cap beneath his helmet and was unharmed. The men then hacked the beast to bits and

---

[183] Reider, Noriko T. "Shuten Dōji: 'Drunken Demon.'" Asian Folklore Studies, vol. 64, no. 2, 2005, pp. 207–31. JSTOR, http://www.jstor.org/stable/30030420. Accessed 25 Sept. 2023.

destroyed it.[184]

William of Newburgh
"It would not be easy to believe that the corpses of the dead should sally from their graves and should wander about to the terror or destruction of the living. Did not frequent examples occurring in our own times suffice to establish this as a warning to posterity, to the truth of which there is abundant testimony." [185]-William of Newburgh, writing in the 12th century.

William of Newburgh was an English historian during the 12th century. His most key work was the History of English Affairs. The tome is still valued and read by historians today as it offers a rare glimpse into everyday life in the 12th century. One such glimpse is into the stories of medieval revenants or vampires.

His works reveal that William of Newburgh was primarily a chronicler of revenant attacks. He collected stories of these events from around England. While this may seem a far cry from being an actual vampire hunter himself, his works offer valuable information pertaining to the identification and manner of disposal for those who would hunt such creatures. One could reasonably draw parallels between the works of Newburgh and those of Dom Calmet a few centuries later.

Conde de Cabreras
Javier Arries, the writer, and researcher of hidden issues has discovered the first official vampire hunter, of which there is documentation. Arries has asserted that he is of Spanish, specifically Valencian, origins.[186] This information is based upon a narrative written by Dom Calmet, a French Benedictine

---

184   Sato, Hiroaki 1995. Legends of the Samurai. Woodstock, NY: Overlook Press.
185   [185] Newburgh, W. (n.d.). William of Newburgh.Book Five. Internet History Sourcebooks: Medieval Sourcebook. https://sourcebooks.fordham.edu/basis/williamofnewburgh-five.asp#5
186   Arries, J. (n.d.). Vampiros Ajusticiados por el conde de cabreras. El Conde de Cabreras. https://www.arries.es/la_cripta/casos/cabreras.html

monk. Dom Calmet held an interest in vampires like Newburgh and wrote extensively upon the subject. The following case is based upon a letter he received from an informant serving in the regiment of Conde de Cabreras.[187]

Conde de Cabreras was a regimental captain during the war between Austrians and Turks in 1715. His fame as a hunter of these creatures arose when Austria conquered regions that his military had occupied and that were watched over by the peasants. One evening, a soldier and one of these men from the field were having dinner when a stranger joined them at the table. To the peasant's surprise, the unexpected visitor was none other than his late father, who had been buried more than 10 years prior.

It was then that the Conde de Cabreras entered the scene, taking it upon himself to clarify the facts. After the peasant's version was verified, he decided to exhume the remains of the father, whose corpse appeared with supposed symptoms of vampirism: an elastic body with red and circulating blood.[188] After confirmation, the body was beheaded and reburied.

The popularity of Conde de Cabreras reached such heights that he was not the only case presented to him. Apparently, he also faced a father, who had died 30 years earlier, who had shown up at lunchtime to suck the blood of his daughter. Another case of vampirism presented itself to him after the death of a woman, which was followed by those of her eldest and youngest sons. After unearthing the woman's body, he observed the same characteristics as in the peasant's father. He decided to cut up the corpse, although the deaths continued, and the woman's remains remained uncorrupted. Case after case, the Conde de Cabreras was unearthing vampires and earning the reputation of hunting the "undead." His technique is trepanning (drilling holes) their temples, burning them, or the then

---

187   Huet, M.H. (1997). Deadly Fears: Dom Augustin Calmet's Vampires and the Rule Over Death. Eighteenth-Century Life 21(2), 222-232. https://www.muse.jhu.edu/article/10415.
188   [188] Calmet, 1850, p33-34

"traditional" beheading.

Sean Manchester

In 1970, Sean Manchester made history by founding the Vampire Research Society and becoming involved in the notorious Highgate Vampire incident in London. Reports of purported supernatural occurrences at Highgate Cemetery in London, England, United Kingdom, during the 1970s resulted in the Highgate Vampire becoming a widely discussed topic in the media.[189]

On 6 February 1970, David Farrant submitted a letter to the Hampstead and Highgate Express in which he stated that while traversing Highgate Cemetery on 24 December 1969, he had observed a "grey figure" which he believed to be supernatural. He further inquired as to whether anyone else had experienced a similar sighting. On the 13th, a number of individuals responded, detailing a variety of spectres said to haunt the cemetery and the adjoining Swains Lane. These apparitions were reported to be a man wearing a hat, a spectral cyclist, a woman in white, a face glaring through the bars of a gate, a figure wading into a pond, a pale gliding form, bells ringing, and voices calling.[190]

Sean Manchester, a vampire hunter, claimed this figure was a vampire. This declaration was quickly latched onto by local media, and a frenzy ensued. At the time, Manchester was the director of an occult investigation bureau, which is now defunct. He became involved, along with Mr. Farrant, in the desecration of graves at the cemetery. The pair, along with other followers, left behind garlic in tombs, removed bodies and burned them, as well as vandalized the cemetery.[191]

---

189 Ellis, B. (1993). The Highgate Cemetery Vampire Hunt: The Anglo-American Connection in Satanic Cult Lore. Folklore, 104(1/2), 13–39. http://www.jstor.org/stable/1260794
190 [190] Hampstead and Highgate Express, 6 February 1970, 26; 13 February 1970, 25; 20 February 1970, 1, 27; 27 February 1970, 6. Cited in Ellis (1993) 20-21; some also in Farrant (1991) 6-8.

For the first two decades, the Society had an open membership and boasted 300 members. However, in 1990, the Research Society decided to restrict membership and focus on practical research. This exclusive group only focuses on paranormal investigations and does not condone any medical disorders, people desiring to be vampires, or non-conventional behavior associated with vampires.

Manchester is not your average vampire enthusiast - he is the Bishop and Primate of the Catholic Apostolic Church of the Holy Grail and takes vampirism seriously as a supernatural occult phenomenon. Despite the media's tongue-in-cheek coverage of him, Manchester is a true believer and believes that those who dabble in vampire culture are playing with fire and promoting evil.

Manchester is determined to spread his message and warn those who may be tempted by the lure of vampire culture. As such, he has dedicated his life to campaigning against the glamorization of vampires and their dark practices. He has even established a charity called 'The Vampire Education and Research Society,' which provides resources for those looking to learn more about the truth and dangers of vampirism. Manchester is on a mission to ensure that no one falls into the trap of believing in vampire myths and instead embraces the reality of this dark practice.

Vampire Slaying Kits

Vampire slaying kits are the quintessential necessity for any would-be vampire hunter. It is claimed that these kits were created for those traveling to Eastern Europe in the late nineteenth century, lending credence to the notion that some made a living off of vampire hunting. Occasionally, one may find displays of vampire killing kits, such as the one to the left from the collection from Ripley's Believe It or Not.

Unfortunately, it is unclear whether these kits were authentic

---

191 [191] Ellis, Bill. Raising the Devil: Satanism, New Religions, and the Media (University Press of Kentucky, 2000), 215-36.

or not. Some experts claim that the earliest of these kits were actually produced in the 1960s or 70s and made to appear antiquated.[192] Yet, looking back at the story of Minamoto no Raiko, it is clear that he traveled with weaponry. This consisted of various blades, such as knives and poisons, as well as blunt instruments like clubs. For all intents and purposes, this is a vampire slaying kit. Yet, it would be quite difficult to travel with such an array of instruments.

According to the British Library, the modern version of the vampire slaying kit was constructed as a souvenir. They were purportedly sold to tourists visiting Eastern Europe in the wake of the popularity of *Dracula*. [193] Naturally, those who sold such kits claimed that they were created for believers as a form of self-protection. These kits were called the Professor Blomberg vampire-slaying kits. However, more recent scholarly research has found that these kits, though using antique trappings, were created closer to the 1930s at the earliest. They were popular during the era of the "Hammer" vampire movies. Hammer vampire movies ran from 1958-1974 and starred the iconic Christopher Lee in the leading role of Dracula.[194]

Vampire Hunters in Fiction

Vampire hunters have become a popular figure in modern fiction and popular culture. Armed with an array of items and weapons designed to exploit the traditional weaknesses of vampires, these hunters are often portrayed as mysterious and dramatic avenging heroes, eccentric extremists, mad scientists, or sometimes a mix of all three. Some are heroic figures, while others are villains from the perspective of the vampire. In some cases, vampire hunters are even bounty hunters, hunting

---

192 [192] Buzwell, G. (2014). History at Stake! The Story Behind Vampire Slaying Kits. British Library. https://blogs.bl.uk/english-and-drama/2014/11/history-at-stake-vampire-slaying-at-the-british-library.html
193 Dracula was published in 1897 by Bram Stoker and immediately became a sensation, prompting Eastern European tourism.
194 [194] Hammer films. Hammer Films. (n.d.). https://www.hammerfilms.com/

vampires for profit. In addition to vampires, these hunters may also hunt werewolves, demons, and other forms of undead. Let's take a look at some of the many vampire hunters in fiction. From mages and cyborgs to members of the clergy and holy orders, this list offers an insight into the various forms a hunter can take.

Van Helsing

A name we all know of is that of Professor Abraham Van Helsing, the fictional character and protagonist from Bram Stoker's 1897 novel Dracula. A known vampire hunter and enemy of Dracula. A well-known and influential archetypal vampire hunter is Professor Abraham Van Helsing, a character in Bram Stoker's 1897 horror novel Dracula, a foundational work in the genre.

Van Helsing is a powerful symbol of good, as he uses science and reasoning to battle the forces of evil. He is ultimately successful in his mission, although he pays a heavy price along the way. His bravery and determination are also inspiring; he never gives up in his fight against evil, even when things seem hopeless. He stands out as a shining example of courage and strength in the face of adversity.

Blade

The half-vampire, half-human vampire hunter from the movies and comic books. Portrayed by Wesley Snipes in the movie adaptation, Blade is a skilled vampire hunter. He teams up with Whistler, a retired vampire hunter and weapons expert, to get revenge on the beasts that killed his mother. The character of Abraham Whistler, portrayed by Kris Kristofferson, was named after the iconic Abraham Van Helsing of *Dracula*.

Blade is a formidable fighter, armed with an array of skills and weapons. He is a master swordsman, able to take on multiple vampires at once, and his arsenal includes ultraviolet stakes, daggers, and guns. He also has the unique ability to sense vampires through their smell and the heat of their bodies.

With his allies by his side, he embarks on a mission to rid the world of vampire evil and protect humanity from their monstrous threats.

Abraham Lincoln

The graphic novel by Seth Grahame-Smith depicts a fictionalized history of the American Civil War with the eponymous 16th president of the United States reimagined as having a secret identity as a lifelong vampire hunter fighting against a caste of vampiric slave owners.

The premise of this novel is truly unique and captivating, as it seamlessly blends history with fantasy. The story follows President Lincoln's journey as he struggles to protect his family and preserve the Union from the vampiric slaveholders. Along the way, he must come face-to-face with powerful adversaries and unexpected allies who are determined to see him succeed. The novel features thrilling action sequences, intense battles, and mesmerizing characters, all of which make for an exciting and unforgettable read.

Frog Brothers

The young brothers from the movie The Lost Boys, the Frog Brothers, were an instant hit with fans when they first appeared in 1987's The Lost Boys. Tasked with helping a new kid in town, Sam Emerson, save his brother Michael from a gang of vampires led by the mysterious David, the Frog Brothers ran the local comic book store for their burned-out parents. But when they weren't at the shop, they were out hunting vamps! Dressed in camouflage shirts and Rambo headbands, the militaristic Frog Boys were determined to take down the coven of vampires that had taken over their town.[195]

---

195 [195] Evry, M. (2022, October 5). How the lost boys' frog brothers kicked off the mainstreaming of comic book culture [exclusive]. /Film. https://www.slashfilm.com/1040372/how-the-lost-boys-frog-brothers-kicked-off-the-mainstreaming-of-comic-book-culture-exclusive/

Buffy Summers

Lastly, let us take a look at the ever-popular Buffy the Vampire Slayer. Created by renowned writer and director Joss Whedon, "Buffy the Vampire Slayer" is an American supernatural drama television series which is based on the 1992 film of the same name.[196] Buffy Summers (played by Sarah Michelle Gellar) is the latest in a long line of Vampire Slayers, chosen by fate to battle against evil forces. But Buffy doesn't want to accept her destiny; she just wants to live a normal life. Fortunately, she's got a Watcher to guide her and a Scooby Gang of loyal friends to help her along the way. Join Buffy on her journey of self-discovery as she learns to embrace her destiny and fight the darkness!

Do You Believe?

While modern myths of vampires are typically traced back to the nineteenth century, the oral folklore can be traced much further back in history. Legends of the undead drinking the blood or eating the flesh of living beings are found in most cultures around the world. Such stories have existed for many centuries. Interestingly, vampires of antiquity were traditionally female. Perhaps this is because of the connection with goddesses in ancient religions. Further, mythology defines women by their sexuality, and what is more attractive and fearsome than a female bloodsucking demon? Through the centuries, vampires have been many things, from undead ghouls to beautiful preternatural creatures, both male and female. Yet, the question of their existence remains. Historically, cultures across the world with seemingly no contact with one another each have similar fabled creatures. Considering this, it is reasonable to assume that within the vampire lore rests a seed of truth.

---

196   PopMatters Staff,. (2011, March 3). Joss Whedon 101: "Buffy the vampire slayer": The movie, PopMatters. PopMatters. https://www.popmatters.com/137558-joss-whedon-101-buffy-the-vampire-slayer-the-movie-2496072873.html

Also Available from Roswell Publishing

Non-Fiction

An Introduction to Magick – Mozinah the Seer
Paranormal Forensic Archeology: Crime Scene Residuals and Ghostly Witnesses – Jonathan Williams, MA
Phantom Vibrations: A History of Ghost Hunting – BR Williams
Send in the Congregation – Rachael Gilliver
Skin O' Our Teeth – Rachael Gilliver
The Mysterious Wold Newton Triangle – Charles Christian
The Human Element – Rachael Gilliver
You Are Not Broken – Rachael Gilliver

Fiction

Death of a Doppelganger – Paul Mackintosh
Letters From Montauk – Rachael Gilliver
The High Price of Fame – Rachael Gilliver

Poetry

A Box at the Back of the Junk Shop – Kate Garrett
Black Ballads – Paul Mackintosh
Deeds – Kate Garrett
Little Gods – Cara L McKee
Mozinah's Book of Fairy Tales – Mozinah the Seer

Printed in Great Britain
by Amazon